How To Work With A Digital Marketing Agency

How To Work With A Digital Marketing Agency

Hassan Bawab

Table of Contents

Chapter Two: Selecting a Digital Marketing Agency..29

Chapter Three: Working with a DMA for Optimum Results..57

Chapter Four: Review for Comprehensiveness 65

ABOUT THE AUTHOR

Hassan Bawab is the founder and CEO of Magic Logix, a Dallas, Texas based integrated marketing agency specializing in customized marketing automation solutions for businesses worldwide.

After the successful launch of Magic Logix in 2004, Mr. Bawab's entrepreneurial ambition continued. He has since developed several other businesses that will debut in 2014. Key to Hassan Bawab's success is his passion for innovation and his ability to incorporate trend-setting technology into the field of web development and marketing automation.

Mr. Bawab is a trusted resource in the industry and often spends his free time as a consultant for Top 1000 Fortune companies. He has been honored as a guest lecturer at global events and conferences, and locally at The University of North Texas, The University of Texas at Dallas, and Southern Methodist University. Hassan has written numerous articles on web development, e-commerce, big data, marketing automation and social media strategies that have become industry dogmas. Hassan is also a well-known speaker and he is a member of National Speakers Association (NSA).

Mr. Bawab holds degrees in Computer Science, Mathematics, Technical Writing and Marketing, in addition to several marketing and programming certifications.

ACKNOWLEDGEMENTS

Apart from the efforts of myself, the success of any project depends largely on the encouragement and guidelines of many others. I take this opportunity to express my gratitude to the people who have been instrumental in the successful completion of this book.

I would like to express my gratitude to the many people who saw me through this book; to all those who provided support, talked things over, read, offered comments, and assisted in the editing and proofreading. Very special thanks to Robert Nahas and his team for the exceptional writing and editorial input.

I would like to thank the design and marketing team at Magic Logix. My wonderful and gifted design team has helped in designing the front and back of the book in addition to the inside images. My marketing team has helped me in extensive research.

Above all I want to thank my lovely wife, Farah and the rest of my family including Dad, Mom, my lovely sister and my great brothers who supported and encouraged me in spite of all the time it took me away from them. It was a long and difficult journey for them.

Special thanks to Chad Burnett, Sam Timalsina and Chris Apaliski–who helped me with this book and the marketing campaign to launch the book at HassanBawab.com

Finally: I thank God everyday for everything he has given me.

Of course it is all about passion and dedication but I love the challenge to make it happen!

ISBN 13: 978-0615971810

ISBN 10: 0615971814

Printed in the United States of America

Many businesses utilize vendors to provide services that, for whatever reason, cannot be done in-house. It stands to reason therefore that vendor management is an important specialized area in larger corporations, as well as a function of management positions in virtually all companies.

Vendor Management encompasses many skills across a broad spectrum; these include an understanding of contacts, relationship-building and negotiations, and the shifting trends in a particular industry and business practices in general. For purposes of this book, the term "vendors" refers to those various enterprises that supply internet marketing, web design, web hosting, and other such services to businesses. "Vendor Management" refers the responsibilities of the client company's Chief Marketing Officer (CMO) and his/her staff in the marketing department.

1. HOW DO NEGOTIATION SKILLS FIT INTO VENDOR MANAGEMENT?

The importance of negotiation skills cannot be overestimated. Although the vendor manager may not be the purchasing agent, he/she often brokers the agreement or leads the negotiations between the parties. There are generally three types of negotiation: passive, principled and aggressive.

Passive Negotiation is where one of the parties makes concessions in order to maintain a good relationship with the other, even if it means he/she will get the raw end of the deal. This person avoids conflict of any kind and usually ends up feeling like he/she has been taken advantage of. This is not generally considered an efficient form of negotiation, but it is a common one. If you have ever been the passive party in a negotiation, you know that it can lead to bitterness and frustration.

On the other end of the spectrum is aggressive negotiation. In this case, the parties see themselves as locked in a battle of wills; for each, the primary goal is winning (and therefore causing the other side to lose). They bicker back and forth, haggling over cost or some other aspect of the deal, each hoping to overcome the other. At the end of the negotiation, the parties are exhausted and the relationship between them suffers. Like passive negotiations, aggressive tactics do not benefit either party in the long term, as they can tarnish a company's reputation and brand.

Principled Negotiations result in fair agreements and are considered the most effective. Unlike lopsided deals created from passive or aggressive tactics, principled negotiations result in the parties coming together for mutual gain. They work through the proposals, using a system of give and take which fosters trust, respect, and a good relationship moving forward.

Effective negotiators also remain abreast of changing approaches to business practices. Negotiation styles have developed and evolved over time in order to adapt to a shifting marketplace, such as an increase in cross-cultural deals. For more a list of recommended books and courses on the art of negotiating, see the Resources section at the end of the chapter.

2. HOW MUCH DO TODAY'S BUSINESSES DEPEND ON VENDORS?

Business has grown more complex, given our increasingly global economy, as well as technological factors such as the Internet, telecommunications, mobile and video technology. Therefore, the number of vendors that any given business requires is greater than ever before, as is the level of dependence that these businesses have on their vendors.

Moreover, an increasing number of businesses are catering to smaller, specialized markets; this is known as niching. For example, the rise of boutiques in the 21st century has led to the falling away and conglomeration of many larger department stores. The result is fewer large businesses and more small and medium-sized businesses that, by their very nature, have no choice but to specialize. This brings about the necessity to pay vendors for the marketing of their products or services.

3. WHAT SKILLS ARE NECESSARY FOR A CAREER IN VENDOR MANAGEMENT?

Typically, companies hire people with prior experience with the roles and responsibilities included in that job description. For example, administrative assistants usually have experience typing, making travel plans and ordering office supplies. It would be natural to assume that the same is true for vendor management positions, but that is not necessarily the case. Progressive companies like Google, Domo, and Magic Logix will, whenever possible, hire people based on their abilities rather than experience. That said, the ability to manage a given vendor is often expected from those in administrative and management roles.

For those interested in a career in vendor management or simply improving their existing skills, there are now courses, certifications, and even a few degree programs. There are countless vendor management consulting firms as well.

4. WHAT TYPES OF VENDORS MIGHT ONE MANAGE FOR THEIR COMPANY?

There are several kinds of vendors that help companies market their products or services. We will cover a few of them here.

Web Designers/Developers:

These days, most companies have an online presence, the cornerstone of which is their website. In fact, your website is often the first impression potential customers have of your company. It is therefore imperative that it projects an image of success, both visually and functionally. It must adhere to your company's mission, product line, and brand, as well as appeal to your target audience.

The web designer/developer must have expertise with the many facets of web design, including graphic design; search engine optimization (SEO); interface design; standardized code and proprietary software; and user experience. He/she must understand the importance of the Home Page in keeping users engaged, as well as clear, compelling copy and easy-to-use navigation.

Hosting:

Once the website has been built, your company will also have to manage the hosting provider, either through an in-house IT department or through a digital marketing agency. To manage a hosting provider, one needs to have specialized knowledge of web technology, and understand the importance of having the necessary bandwidth and back-end functionality, such as database size.

These days, people rarely have the patience or desire to wait for anything—let alone a slow website. That's why bandwidth--which determines how quickly a computer can connect to a website—is so critical. If a potential customer/client finds it takes too long to connect to your website, you may lose that sale. Your bandwidth must be large enough to readily download all the data you want to present to your client without them having to wait.

The back-end involves includes all that activity that assembles your website and markets it from behind the scenes. You want to be able to update your website from time to time to match the activities of your company. When a customer buys something using the shopping cart, you want to receive the correct data connected with that sale so the buyer gets the product he wanted at the current price. If you make any changes to products, prices, or any other data, you want to convey this new information to the public as quickly as possible; this is done through your back office. This is especially important for time sensitive promotional and seasonal marketing.

Understanding traffic activity, and forecasts of traffic activity as they relate to a website's hosting capacity, is also critical. This lets you know what aspects of your marketing are working and what needs to be changed in order to attract more customers. You must be able to gauge how effective your efforts in driving traffic to your website and turning them into buying customers.

Another very important requirement is the ability to contact the hosting provider should your website break down. Down-time can cause multimillion dollar losses and even irreversible damage to your business. That's why there are governance, compliance and risk regulations and programs for financial and medical institutions. It is therefore important to have a 24/7 hosting services provider, as well as a good working relationship with that provider. When dealing with the hosting provider, your vendor manager must also be knowledgeable about data back-up and disaster recovery.

Marketing:

Throughout this book we will be discussing the benefits of hiring an outside vendor to handle your online marketing needs. A full-service digital marketing agency can assist you with everything from branding and lead generation to social networking, and analytics (i.e. search engine ranking). Given the rapidity with which technology is evolving, as well as the need to always stay one step ahead of your competitors, it make sense to leave the marketing to the experts, thus, freeing up your staff to deal with the business itself. That said, if you do hire a marketing company, you will still need to oversee their work and otherwise manage them, just as you would any other vendor. Most importantly, you must be able communicate easily with them regarding your marketing strategy and be sure that they are providing measurable results (meaning their work is increasing your business).

5. WHAT IS THE IMPORTANCE OF WORKING WELL WITH VENDORS AND THIRD PARTIES?

Vendor relationships rise to the level of quasi-partnerships in the commercial environment; and often a company will not reveal to its clients what part of the operation is handled by a vendor and what is managed by in-house staff. Whatever the case, the quality of the vendor's service is paramount to the operations of the company.

Even a seemingly insignificant item could hold up service if not delivered properly. If a bank does not work with the financials or a lawyer does not provide necessary information for a contract, services may be delayed or goods may be held on the manufacturing line.

Understanding a vendor's specialty is only one aspect of vendor management. In order to ensure the timely and accurate delivery of goods and services, one must get along well with the vendor. This relationship often yields benefits that can provide a competitive edge, such as price discounts, exclusive deals and agreements, and joint barrier to entry development.

Vendors often give referrals as well, which is another reason to utilize specialized vendor management. In most cases, the potential referral business is too important to trust vendor management to an unqualified individual or firm. However, vendor management is not "one size fits all'. An experienced vendor manager may come with a referral base, or they may be able to open doors when approaching a new vendor in just the right way.

Vendors can also provide publicity. Many collect success stories and testimonials from qualified partners, which they pass along to the public or other companies they deal with. They use their websiteks to share testimonials, marketing collateral such as brochures, fliers, handouts, website content, blog articles, press releases and social media.

It typically takes specialized knowledge to manage relationships with technology vendors. Given the ever-evolving and complex nature of this area, the vendor must be well-versed in technological lingo and the latest advancements in order to communicate effectively.

The intricacies of working with information technology

have led to multiple specializations, many necessitating an almost savant-like facility with knowledge. One must be able to keep up with a constant flow of information regarding education, information intake, industry conference attendance, news reviews, and research and innovation activity.

A company's digital presence is critically important to its success. Whether it is an extension of a physical presence, or—for online businesses—the only presence, it is the face the company presents to the world.

6. HOW TO WORK SUCCESSFULLY WITH A DIGITAL MARKETING AGENCY (DMA)

A digital marketing agency that really understands the needs of their clients is worth its weight in gold. However, it is the job of the client company to provide all the information the DMA needs to do its job consistently.

The content management system (CMS) serves as the holder of the site content; therefore, it must be structured, integrated, designed and developed in such a way that accurately and completely reflects the company's image, identity, brand and product or service offerings.

The CMS needs to be as scalable and expandable as the client company needs, and in the ways that they need. A DMA that understands the value of CMS scalability forecasts will provide the most effective results to grow the client's business.

The website design needs to reflect exactly and precisely what the client company desires to communicate; it must also be variable to reflect the image and identity of the client. The design needs to be in sync with the company's character; therefore, no matter how good the relationship is between the DMA and the client, it is highly advisable that both parties have written documentation regarding the client's brand and the interpersonal connection, resulting in a clear understanding of nonverbal design goals and visions.

DMAs often integrate customer relationship management tools—or CRMs—into CMSs so that sales teams can compile information about prospects and customers into an orderly format. The CRM uses several channels including social media, email, telephone, internet searches and direct mail in order to measure their client's various campaigns. This system can track who visits your website, up to the moment they become buyers. They can also be used as a call center to direct customers to agents, as well as to set up appointments for your clients.

Salesforce is a common and popular CRM. DMAs that understand their client can do a better job of customizing the integration of customer and prospect data into the integration and design of the CMS and CRM connection.

For B2B companies, one of the most valuable—and complex--digital integration projects is the integration of marketing automation tools, also known as Turbo fuel for B2B businesses.

7. WHAT IS A MARKETING AUTOMATION TOOL?

The marketing automation tool is arguably the most sophisticated development for B2B prospect and client sales and data management. Marketing automation tools automate as much of a website's digital marketing as possible, maximizing cost savings, systematization, and research insights to facilitate better marketing efforts around non-automated activity. They automate repetitive tasks such as email marketing and tracking the behavior of interested visitors to see what products or services they are interested in. They also record which social media links they followed so that a more accurate program can be developed to specifically target the interests of the potential buyer.

Since the value of a single sale to B2B businesses can run in the thousands or even millions of dollars, lead generation, nurturing, qualifying and management are highly important. Sales executives take great care to see proper follow-through activity occurs on behalf of their sales representatives.

The tools provide insight into lead quality, automate online lead nurturing in the CMS, and facilitate sales representatives' follow-up actions by working with the CRM. Marketo, Eloqua and Genius are examples of marketing automation tools. These tools do not operate automatically from the start, but need to be integrated into a CMS and CRM.

8. WHAT DO MARKETING AUTOMATION TOOLS DO?

The integration is complex by nature because it involves determining the definition of a quality lead, as well as the prioritizing of the leads' features and characteristics to enable automatic lead scoring and ranking. Marketing automation tool integration also requires the identification of those marketing actions that can and should be automated from the website or digital interface in order to maximize leads.

Amazon is an excellent example of how marketing automation tools work and what they do on the front end of a website. When a B2B visitor views the website, the website with a marketing automation tool presents individualized content for that particular viewer.

Marketing automation tools maximize a site visitor's user experience with the brand, while allowing real time evaluation of the effectiveness of marketing and site content.

9. WHY DO B2B BUSINESSES USE MARKETING AUTOMATION TOOLS?

Although B2B businesses vary widely, the benefits of marketing automation tools include some commonalities:

- Increased speed, smoothness and accuracy in execution of marketing campaigns

- Higher quality of insights from analytics

- Better working relationships between sales departments and marketing departments

- Improved quality of leads

- Reduced labor needs in development and execution of marketing campaigns

10. WHAT ARE THE MAIN CONSIDERATIONS WHEN USING MARKETING AUTOMATION TOOLS?

There are five key practical insights on integrating marketing automation tools:

- Start with as clean and clear a database as possible.

  Before beginning, be sure to merge, purge and filter out duplicates, leads that are no longer active and unproductive data; otherwise the system will be flooded with useless information. You won't have the correct data to operate with, and this will give you a false picture of your marketing success or failures. From this, you might formulate incorrect marketing programs that lead to loss of revenue.

- Determine what an optimal lead looks like.

  What are the measurable characteristics? Would you recognize a potential customer or client

- How would a lead be scored so as to be ranked as a sales-ready lead?

  Which criteria are absent or present? Make a list of those criteria that you feel are necessary to evaluate whether a lead is ready to buy. These should be used in the process of scoring them, using the automatic marketing tools.

- How many different sales process flows are there when a visitor views your company's site?

  What are the steps of each sales process flow? Which steps make sense to automate and which steps do not? The who, what, where and when of the sale come into play in developing logical, usable, sensible sales flows.

- How is your content mapped or how should it be mapped, or does it need to be developed in order to be mapped?

  Does your site include content that leads the visitor to the action they would like to pursue that is appropriate to the stage of the sales cycle from which they come? Does the content inform? Does the content address a common question? Does the content invoke a reader to desire to act and make a contact or fill out a form? Each sales process flows need multiple kinds of content and each flow usually requires both a unique and a shared content relative to other flows.

- What is the cost and integration time of the marketing automation tools?

  The cost and integration time of marketing automation tools vary on a case-by-case basis. Tools are sold as a software, either as a service or a perpetual license. Your company can pay it all up front or make monthly payments.

In addition to knowledge of your business and the selection of a fitting marketing automation tool, one must take the proper care to integrate it in the most customized way possible. Marketing automation tool installation is a tailor-made business and requires a seamless relationship between the company and the DMA. A system, set of processes, people and communication channels comprise a critical path to success.

Actian, a Fortune 1000 company client is a great e case study on a large B2B marketing automation tool integration of Marketo.

- How about consumer products companies?

For B2C businesses or consumer goods and services companies, site development and promotions have to impact millions of people. With Marriott and FedEx, Magic Logix had to take the finest points of the brand image into consideration. When dealing with a brand identity, it does not matter whether the client company is large or small--the utmost care must be taken to achieve brand consistency.

We have spoken much about the relationship between the client company and the DMA; however, regardless of the relationship, the promotional plan for a consumer website and digital presence must be laid out in detail. Systems and processes for inter-company connection and communication are clear and well worked out and understood in advance, as well as adhered to and respected.

The products and complementary product lines need to be designed in integrity with both the company brand and the individual brands they represent; this is why effective communication with the DMA is so important. Imagine, for example, the kinds of issues FedEx and Marriott would have had if their relationships with Magic Logix were not of the best quality during the digital marketing project management of their websites.

RECOMMENDED RESOURCES:

Start with No, by Jim Camp (2007)

Getting to Yes, by Fisher and Ury (1991)

Winning, by Jack Welch and Suzy Welch (2005)

Chapter One
KNOW YOUR COMPANY'S PURPOSE IN HIRING A DMA

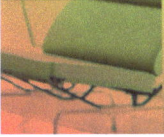

The reasons for hiring a Digital Marketing Agency (DMA) are different from one company to the next. Deciding to work with a DMA, based solely on convincing, savvy ad copy or a favorable comment from somebody or any other high-level, non-systematic approach, is not enough. In fact, it is a risky and reckless approach to take, because it has the potential to be destructive to your company.

Significantly wasted company time, energy and income are the status quo for far too many companies. Such detrimental outcomes must be avoided at all cost – and they can be!

There are aspects specific to each company, based on its needs and intentions. The specific aspects of your company must be "clearly" understood in order to make the best choice and get the most impressive results possible for your continued expansion and prosperity.

Before you select a digital marketing agency, it is important to determine what your company needs and wants. It would be difficult to even have an advantageous dialogue with an agency before this step were done. Thus, proper research and an in-depth awareness of your company's fundamental business strategy must be accomplished and clarified before any shopping around is conducted, much less decisions made. The essential points that need to be considered follow in this chapter.

1. WHAT IS YOUR COMPANY'S UNIQUE SELLING PROPOSITION?

Why do customers or clients buy from your company? What makes each of your products and/or services valuable to your clientele? Examine each product and service your company offers and determine their "attractive value." You should know the answer for each one.

Understanding who the people are that manage the different areas of your company is important too. Who is in charge of the sales division? Who is the CMO? Who oversees your website? Which other executives and managers are responsible for your company's products and services? You will want to know this kind of data and have it at your fingertips to share with the DMA that you work with. This way, they can service you much better, allowing them to do their job most effectively in helping to raise your company's statistics in a significant and seemingly miraculous way.

Take Actian, for example. Actian is a leading data management company that deals in big data-related software. Their clients are businesses that include the Fortune 500 companies and the larger corporations that use big data. Actian, like most other large corporations, has product executives and managers assigned to be responsible for each product that they offer. The CMO is ultimately responsible for the website; as is the case in many companies because the site is a marketing instrument. The CMO is able to ensure that Magic Logix is always apprised of strategic marketing presentation and product development information.

Another example is the CMO of FedEx Global, who is responsible for effectively communicating to Magic Logix their strategic content and design information pertaining to FedEx's brand identity and image. Magic Logix's ability to make sure that the consumer visitor information can be monitored and analyzed is of paramount significance.

With such coordination, things can work smoothly and to everyone's greatest advantage and ideal outcome.

2. WHAT IS YOUR COMPANY'S BASIC BUSINESS STRATEGY AND SWOT ANALYSIS?

SWOT stands for Strength, Weaknesses, Opportunities and Threats. It is a great analysis tool to use for evaluating a business venture or project. From there, the objectives for the company can be determined and a successful basic business strategy drawn up.

Strengths

Strengths are those characteristics of the company that give it an advantage over other similar companies. These can include the technology used by the company, the company management, the distribution of the products, profitability in a certain area, capacity and even the sales. There may be other strengths such as proprietary assets, including patents, trademarks or copyrights. Even a strong reputation, a good brand name, premium pricing and exclusive access to resources are possible strengths.

Weaknesses

Weaknesses are characteristics of a company that put them at a disadvantage as compared to other competing/ related companies. A high cost structure would definitely be a weakness as well as a lower-than-desired profitability in a certain section of the company. Competitor activity could also vie for sales in a particular manner that is more successful than your own. Even the absence of the strengths listed above can be considered weaknesses. All these things can diminish the viability of your own company.

Opportunities

Opportunities are situations that present themselves, which a company can use to its advantage. They can be used to strengthen the regulatory environment of the company as well as strengthen a trend. New products may present themselves as well. These are all opportunities that are worthwhile to take into consideration when analyzing the business.

Threats

On the other hand, threats, which are elements in the environment that could potentially cause trouble for the company, include situations in the regulatory environment that change for the worse when a new legislature is put in place. Threats can also include unfulfilled needs of the customer as well as the competitors' ability to meet those needs in comparison.

From this analysis, you will be able to draw up your company's general business strategy, using one of the following four main types of strategies:

S-O

This strategy pursues the opportunities that correspond to the company's strengths.

W-O

In this strategy, the company works on overcoming weaknesses to pursue opportunities.

S-T

A company using this strategy applies its strengths to shield against threats.

W-T

This strategy defends its weaknesses against possible threats.

Example: Marketing Automation Tools

Actian's marketing automation tools corresponded to using their strengths to maximize opportunities, or align with S-O strategic approach. The content created by them automatically matches itself specifically to the individual preferences of the particular B2B visitor that interacts predominantly with their site, based on the ever updated information, analytics and developments.

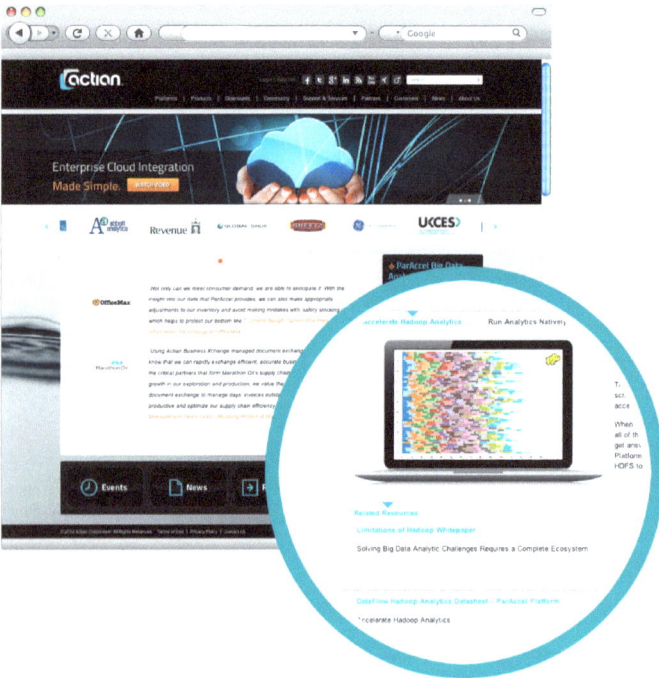

3. DO YOU KNOW YOUR COMPANY'S HISTORY OVER THE LAST THREE TO FIVE YEARS?

Before speaking with a digital marketing agency, it is important to know your company's history for the past three to five years, including its previous goals and resources.

The more information, the better. It's alright if your company doesn't have the information, but having such data will help your DMA to better design, develop and digital-market your project because it can build upon any past knowledge. For example, consider knowing the following before talking to an agency:

- What new and unique visitors have visited your website?
- What were the conversion rates of leads to inquiries?
- What were the conversion rates to purchases?
- What site viewing and visiting patterns developed between pages?
- Were there any content preferences by market segments?
- What were the sources of the visitors?
- Which promotions were successful and what were the lessons learned?
- Did you have any event activity with your online marketing?
- What newsletter activity were you engaged in with online marketing?
- Was there any app activity with your online marketing?
- What was your automated marketing tool experience?
- What email marketing activity successes did you experience and what were the lessons learned?

Example: Marketing Automation Tools

In the case of Actian, all of the above information had to be assessed and known before and during the integration of the marketing automation tools into the Salesforce CRM and their Joomla CMS. Actian's marketing automation tool integration was especially complex due the nature of the size of their company, the complexity of their innovative, cutting-edge, technological product-lines and the size of their client base.

The integration has been a great success because Actian was diligent in providing all needed information in a timely manner, and communicated (and continues to communicate) in a systematic way in alignment with Magic Logix's processes.

4. HOW DOES YOUR COMPANY'S BRAND ASSETS, LOGO FORMS, TAG LINE, ETC., FIT TOGETHER TO SUPPORT YOUR COMPANY'S OVERALL BRAND?

Another important step to take before speaking to a DMA is to have or take an inventory of all of your company's brand assets, logo forms, tag lines, any supporting graphics or imagery, style guides, product or services lines and show how they fit together to support your company's overall brand. Once you have your inventory, you can share them with your DMA. You will want to know how to present the items first, and a style guide that defines all of your branding guidelines would be very useful for the DMA. Then you will want to know how they want you to share this data with them. There are several file-sharing systems you can use online such as Box.net, Openbox.com or even a shared drive, not to mention others you might find.

5. WHAT ARE THE COMPANY'S CULTURAL VALUES THAT DEFINE THE IDENTITY OF THE BRAND?

Do you have a mission statement and a vision statement that help to brand your company? If so, be prepared to provide the digital marketing agency with these so they are able to get to know your company's identity better. The better they get to know who you are, the better job they will do in marketing your company and its products.

How about any marketing researches you may have done? These show insights that will guide your brand presentation and is important to share with the DMA.

Once you have found the right DMA for you, allow them time to review and present their suggestions. When they make those suggestions, take the time to consider them and arrive at a goal and resource commitment that centers on your company's success within reasonable parameters that the DMA is confident it can deliver.

The objective in determining your company's strategic information as much as possible in advance of selecting and meeting with the digital marketing agency is manifold. First there is a cost savings in time and money by doing your company's homework upfront. If the agency had to do it for your company, the cost would be unquestionably greater.

Secondly, at the end of the day, your company directs the digital marketing agency based on that information, and hence should be the master of it.

Thirdly, if the strategy guiding the company's course is not determined by the company, who knows its own interests best, that strategy is not going to be based on the most accurate understanding of your company's interests.

Also consider recommendations from outside companies such as consulting firms and digital marketing agencies, as they are usually highly accurate and helpful in the particular areas of expertise, but ultimately, decide your company's overall business strategy internally. Do not ever fully outsource strategy.

Example: Marketing Automation Tools

Actian Corporation took many of Magic Logix's recommendations in how to best install the Marketo automated marketing tools, yet Actian was the determining party for its own business strategy.

Example: Consumer Products Goods Company

FedEx Office determined their strategy and that strategy affected all work done for them in every aspect of the digital marketing solutions that Magic Logix provided.

6. THE CLEARER THE TARGET, THE EASIER IT IS TO HIT!

Crystal clear knowledge of your company's purpose for hiring the digital marketing agency helps all parties see, aim, and hit the target. That is the simplicity of it. The more sophisticated the company, the clearer and more definitively they know and can assess their own needs.

When a client company comes to the table with a clear understanding of their main purpose in hiring a digital marketing agency, the agency can more rapidly and more effectively deliver the digital marketing solutions service.

Actian usually provides regular updates for their new products, their news, and their new company developments. The SEO which is a part of the design, is always able to be maximized to its fullest because of Actian's outstandingly prompt and meticulous attention to constant communication with Magic Logix.

It's the responsibility of the client company to make sure all of their employees, especially any who come into contact with the digital marketing agency, know their company's brand. It is also important, in order to maximize the efficiency of communications and avoid any unnecessary confusion, that all relevant employees know the client company's purpose in hiring the digital marketing firm.

7. VISUAL STRATEGY DEVELOPMENT AND COMMUNICATIONS TECHNIQUES: TREASURE MAPPING

Techniques to help your company identify its purpose and where it wishes to go include mapping, where senior management draws and maps its vision as though it were creating its own secret map to a buried treasure in a location where only they know.

After the map is done, see where the digital marketing best helps the company get to where it wants to go, and add it in or make a separate map including the digital marketing effort.

Feel free to share that with your digital marketing agency. Part of the magic of creating excellent strategy that leads to excellent execution, is having fun along the way and getting creative with it!

Game version of your strategy

Try a game version description of your strategy where each key executive is responsible for the instructions or description of part of the game.

After the game instructions are complete, see where the digital marketing best helps the company win, and add it in or make a separate sheet including the digital marketing effort. Feel free to share that with your digital marketing agency.

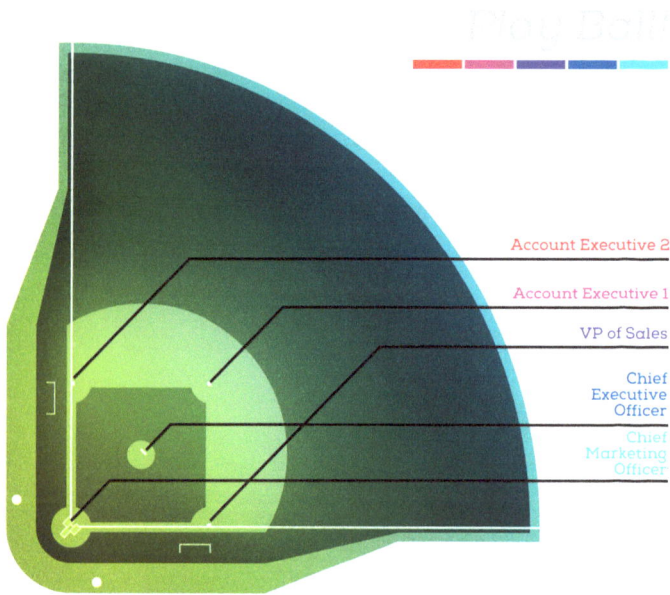

Using the image-based strategy development and communications techniques helps open up creative channels in corporate employees to facilitate and maximize their work with the digital marketing agency.

Example: Marketing Automation Tools

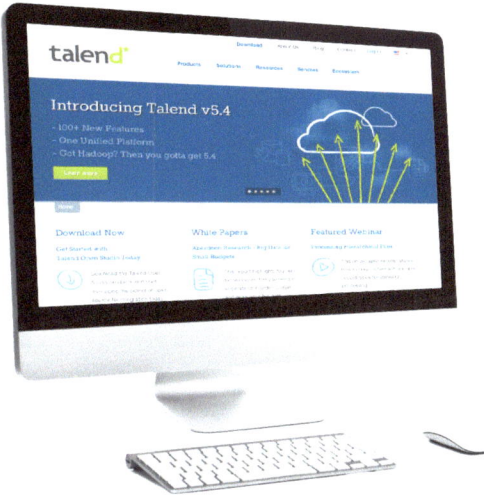

Magic Logix enabled Talend to streamline, automate, and measure marketing tasks and workflows, so they can increase operational efficiency and grow revenue faster.

Chapter Two

SELECTING A DIGITAL
MARKETING AGENCY

There are several different kinds of digital marketing agencies. There are web development firms that set up your website; web design firms to design your websites; social media firms to promote your website through Twitter, Google Plus, Facebook, LinkedIn, and other social networks; mobile app firms that help develop your website apps for mobile devices such as smart phones, tablets, and other electronic devices; database development firms that set up your data collection and management systems; and firms that do all of the above such as Drupal, Joomla or Magento, which are open-source web development platforms using open-source languages.

We will take a look at agencies that cover all of digital marketing, but first, what is open-source language and an open-source web development platform?

1. "OPEN SOURCE" EXPLAINED

Open Source VS Proprietary Source Codes

Computers use programs that give them instructions on what to do, and how. These programs are written in a certain source code (or language) that the computer can interpret.

There are two different kinds of source code in vogue

today. The proprietary software uses a source code that cannot be viewed or altered. A Digital Marketing Agency will use this to set up a website and market it, but you, as the client, will not have access to it to alter anything. In a way, this protects the DMA against any alteration to the website which may counter what they are setting up and building upon. On the other hand, the open source software uses a code that can be viewed and altered by anyone. There are advantages to each.

If you don't have the skills to alter the source code and want to save time, the DMA that uses a proprietary source code is the agency of choice because they can change the website for you. However, if you do have the skills and want to edit the source code yourself, the open source is a better choice. Even if you don't have the skills, you can hire or contract someone to edit it for you in this last case. Still, there is potentially an ideal option that suits the majority. This is discussed next.

Advantages of Using Open Source Language

Due to the vast size of the community that does know open source languages, it is highly recommend-ed that companies use a digital marketing agency that works with them. The numerous advantages include:

1. Since most software releases contain bugs, it's easier to edit the software within the open source code in order to fix them.

2. There's better security with the open source code system.

3. You can customize the application to meet your specific needs.

4. It's easy to translate the language of the software

interface, making your website more international in a global market.

5. By using open source, you avoid being locked in, which occurs when you use proprietary software. When you are locked in, it is more difficult to use other vendors, and you can end up paying a higher price for the digital marketing agency.

6. You reduce the danger of a possible vendor collapse or the discontinuation of a product. Since proprietary source code is owned, it may stop being available, supported, or updated when a commercial vendor goes bust. This can cause a very expensive and difficult situation for your company when you need to switch to a different website building and marketing product.

7. Using an open source code help you improve your skills.

8. You can become part of a community of programmers, which can help you establish reputation and respect, not to mention valuable experience.

9. All of the above increases cost efficiency as well.

Source: http://www.oss-watch.ac.uk/resources/whoneedssource

An example of a proprietary software coding approach is that put out by Microsoft as .Net. This platform enables the user to create increased interactive websites.

One of the advantages of proprietary coding is that a support contact is usually included with the agreement. At one point in time, all the advantages listed above for open source coding, were advised to be the unique benefits of proprietary coding approaches, but that is an antiquated statement today.

All of the advantages that have been touted about increased security and quality are no longer unique to proprietary software when the open source software evolved to become mainstream.

2. THE MAIN PLAYERS FOR EACH TYPE INCLUDING STRENGTHS AND CAUTIONS

According to Gartner Inc., there are four main players that we should look at here, along with their strengths and cautions. These are leaders, challengers, niche players and visionaries. You will see how they are placed in the diagram of the Magic Quadrant put together by Gartner below. Let's take a look at each one with examples of each and then we'll have a look at what criteria is used to evaluate the companies and place them on the quadrant.

THE MAIN PLAYERS

Leaders

The leaders are those companies with the greatest ability to execute the marketing plans and projects as well as having the greatest completeness of vision, as shown by the diagram. IBM Interactive qualifies as a Leader in that it delivers high quality work throughout the world and demonstrates strong skills in creative services and user experience. Magic Logix falls into this category as well.

Challengers

Challengers are those DMAs that are very capable of providing excellent service and products in the digital marketing arena but are limited in the completeness of their vision. For example, Draftfcb, as a Challenger, is known for expertise in brand and multicultural insight. But it has global account management issues as it endeavors to integrate the digital with traditional businesses.

Digitas is also a Challenger, with its comprehensive management in the field of digital programming and insight into their customers' needs and wants. However, they fall short on their completeness of vision due to their limited reach. They have a majority of clients in the U.S., U.K. and France instead of reaching out into other global areas for markets.

Visionaries

Those companies that demonstrate a completeness of vision but lack in the ability to execute the projects as well are labeled as Visionaries. As they move into being able to function more fully in marketing effectiveness and efficiency, they can move up to being Leaders. Accenture Interactive is considered a Visionary because it operates on a global scale, is strong in being able to measure the effectiveness of marketing, and reports positive increases in lead-to-deal conversion rates as well as a decrease in campaign cycles, marketing costs and marketing acquisition costs. However, they are weak in creative services, experience design and campaign ideation.

Digital@Oglivy is another Visionary. They are capable in dealing with identity, brand and PR, as well as creativity. Their global reach is a strong point and their social outreach is of leader quality. And although they focus on digitally enabled direct marketing, management of campaigns and analytics, they lack the system integration skills, application development and architecture that Leaders have.

Nichers

The fourth player is the Nichers who specialize in a certain niche rather than full service. They may concentrate on website building or social networking, for example. Perhaps they cater more to a certain industry such as the auto industry

or the medical field. They become an expert in what they do and a company looking only for service in a specific niche rather than full service may want to choose this type of player.

Meredith Xcelerated Marketing is a Nicher. They are expert at content creation and marketing and specializes in automotive and entertainment. Another plus point for MXM is that it is expanding into a global market. On the other hand, it is limited as far as strategic services and technology go. It also uses a less flexible billing approach that other agencies.

MAGIC QUADRANT FOR GLOBAL DIGITAL MARKETING AGENCIES

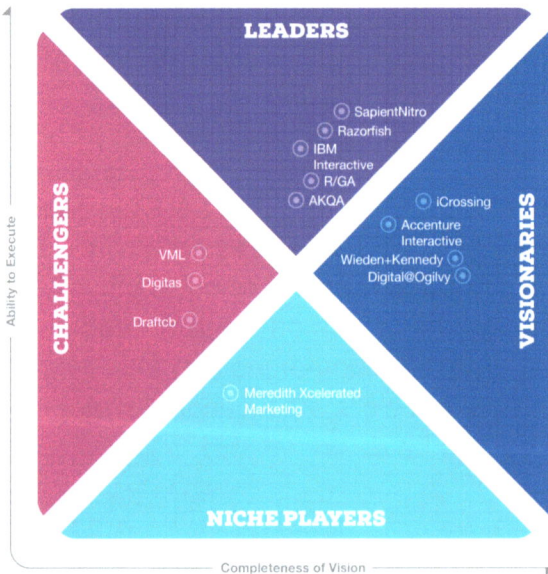

LEADERS

CHALLENGERS

VISIONARIES

NICHE PLAYERS

Ability to Execute

Completeness of Vision

As of October 2012

SapientNitro
Razorfish
IBM Interactive
R/GA
AKQA
iCrossing
Accenture Interactive
Wieden+Kennedy
Digital@Ogilvy
VML
Digitas
Draftcb
Meredith Xcelerated Marketing

CRITERIA USED TO PLACE DMAS ON THIS QUADRANT

The various DMAs are evaluated according to a list of criteria and thus you may find that the quadrant will change from year to year or from evaluation to evaluation, depending on the changes within the agencies themselves. Here are those criteria that is used to evaluate the digital marketing agencies.

Criteria to evaluate ability to execute are as follows:

1. The agency's ability to execute their services to the client. This includes such things as what core goods and services are offered by the vendor.

2. The agency's overall viability. The overall financial health is taken into consideration as well as their financial and practical success and a prediction of whether the vendor will continue to invest in the product or continue to offer it in the future.

3. The ability of the vendor in its presales activities, including pricing, negotiation, presales support and overall effectiveness of the sales channel.

4. What market response and track record they have including their ability to respond, be flexible and achieve success as a competitor as opportunities come up.

5. How the vendor executes the marketing, whether the programs show clarity, quality, creativity and efficacy in delivering the organization's message to the market, thus influencing that market to purchase their product or service.

6. The experience of the client/customer with the DMA with regard to relationships and services or programs that help the client become more successful such as technical support, account support and even customer support programs and other ancillary tools.

7. The DMA's ability to meet its goals and commitments effectively and efficiently on a regular basis.

Criteria to evaluate the completeness of vision include these things:

1. The ability of the DMA to understand just what the buyers will buy according to their wants and needs and translate them into services and products.

2. The marketing strategy that DMA uses to market the client's products or services in that the messages are consistently communicated throughout the website, in their advertising, customer programs, etc.

3. The kind of sales and marketing strategy are used to sell the products in the appropriate network.

4. The vendor's approach to product development and delivery.

5. How sound and logical the vendor's underlying business proposition is.

6. How the vendor meets the specific needs of the individual with resources, offerings and skills.

7. The innovation of the vendor towards such elements as capital for investment, consolidation or even synergistic layouts of resources, etc.

8. The global outreach program used whether directly or through other channels, partners, etc., depending on what is appropriate for that market or geography.

3. HOW TO ASSESS THE FIT OF A DIGITAL MARKETING AGENCY

You may wonder how to determine which digital marketing agency to use. You probably realize that it's important to choose the one that will complement your business and bring prosperity to you through their marketing. The wrong one chosen can mean the difference between profit and loss. But how does one really know which one when there are so many? What should one look for in a digital marketing agency?

There are actually eight main factors that determine if an agency is the right fit for your company and will help you build a successful business. These eight are personalities, process orientation, processes, brand character, sophistication, urgency, commitment and technology. Let's take a look at each factor in more detail.

Personalities

The DMA companies must have a staff of personalities that work well enough together to facilitate effective communication about the digital marketing activity. If people do not have personalities that can work together, work cannot be done well – a basic consideration, but one that would be wrong to not list and mention for its value. In turn, the staff of the DMA must also be compatible with the marketing staff of your own company so that decisions can be made and carried out without dissension. There is nothing more frustrating, not to mention time wasting, than misunderstandings and disagreements. So personality is an important factor.

Process Orientation

The level of formality and process orientation makes a huge impact on the way a client company and a digital marketing agency work together. Process orientation has to do with "how" things are done rather than just following the leadership of a boss as is done in a company built upon hierarchy. This involves staff working as team members on the company projects, as well as the ability to be open- minded and, if needed, follow a new path in achieving the end product. A digital marketing agency that is highly process-oriented such as Magic Logix will not work well with a company whose employees are not comfortable working with a process-oriented setup.

Magic Logix uses its SCRUM- and AGILE-based C3-DPO (Client 3-Dimensional Plus Operation), or client centered 3D-plus operandi approach to project management, client intake, account management, and all efforts and initiatives on which it endeavors to embark. (Both SCRUM AND AGILE are new method approaches that follow a certain framework, utilizing process orientation to get a project done within a specified time.) We will take up C3-DPO shortly.

Magic Logix's processes, being based on AGILE and SCRUM, are flexible. However, there is still structure and order to ensure progress and the attainment of goals within a desired timeframe.

Look at your own company and see how it is structured. Do you have a hierarchy of leaders down to workers kind of working arrangement or do you make use of the process orientation format? How about the DMA that you are looking at using? Would your staff be comfortable with the degree of process orientation that the DMA uses?

Processes

Look at the processes your company uses and then ask about the processes the digital marketing agency uses. You will want your project management processes to fit well with those of the DMA. For example, Six Sigma, PMP, AGILE, SCRUM (all techniques for managing projects) and similar process approaches to project management fit well together. These approaches also fit well with approaches like Magic Logix's C3-DPO, explained at the end of this chapter.

Brand Character

Ascertain the similarities in the overall brand character of your company and that of your prospective digital marketing agencies.

For example, the Magic Logix brand is about uplifting, supporting and building its clients. The logo is deliberately open and lifting a sphere, representing our client as well as the convergence of creativity, technology and online marketing that Magic Logix develops for them, with them and around them.

Innovation and creativity along with precision and deliberateness are hallmarks of Magic Logix. Leadership can only be followed if it is clearly defined, and as a leader in the industry, Magic Logix prides itself on building leaders among its clients.

Sophistication

There is a spectrum of sophistication. Do not clash by hiring a firm that is the opposite of your company's comfort. It will affect your working relationship, which is fundamental to your success.

The way to determine sophistication is through the brand presentation, collateral, bios, processes, cases, and the interactions your company has with the digital marketing agency. Their reputation and social media presence are also factors.

Urgency

Both companies need to be in agreement on the time line, and that time line must be spelled out clearly. They each need to know where they are going and when. This lends prediction to the project and security for both companies.

Commitment

There will be surprises and changes along the way with any digital marketing project. However, commitment is the determining factor as to whether the project will continue with highest level of quality consistently or not. As well, reputation and cases, along with your impression of personal interaction, will be an effective gauge.

Technology

The coding languages, the technology used by digital marketing agency2 and your company's technology should match or be complementary. For example, .NET does not work easily with open source programming.

4. FIVE BASIC RFP (REQUEST FOR PROPOSAL) DATA ELEMENTS FOR DIGITAL MARKETING AGENCIES – PERTINENT POINTS RE: QUALIFICATIONS OF A DMA TO MEET YOUR COMPANY'S NEEDS

There are five pertinent points to keep in mind when you are ready to ask various digital marketing agencies to submit a proposal to your company. These are important because there are many different agencies to service you and you will want to get the right fit for your company. Getting the right DMA to meet your marketing needs will make a difference in the success of that marketing. Let's take a look at these five points so that you can qualify the agencies that you request proposals from.

Your Company's Needs

Spell out your company's needs as understood by your company. Make sure they are precise and complete, as you will want the DMA to fulfill those needs exactly. Don't leave this to guesswork by the DMA. Otherwise, you might get a product or service that you don't want, or wasted time in them trying to figure out what you really do want. Wasted time spells out lost income and that's not good for your company.

Your DMA's Skills and Experience

Request relevant DMA staff skills and experience. You want to know what your DMA staff can do. Will they be able to provide the end product that you want in your website, your marketing and the brand image you want to portray?

Request relevant DMA experience and project examples. How about finding out how long the DMA has been in business. Have they serviced companies

comparable to your own? Examine their project examples. Are they of the quality you desire? Can they deliver in the timeframe that you need?

The DMA's Approach to Marketing and Website Design

Request DMA provide their approach and recommendations based on your company needs. You will want to know just how the DMA will tackle your website, your marketing, your social media, etc. The DMA should be able to provide what approach they will take and their recommendations as well. Good com-munication depends on this step in order for the DMA to competently provide you with the service you need.

Scope and Time Information

Request scope and time information as a starting point for further discussion upon follow up. This will give you prediction so that you can plan your own company's programs and actions. And you can then prepare questions you might have regarding your website, marketing, etc., for the next discussion.

5. WHEN TO ARRANGE FOR A CONSULTATION

As soon as your company has determined a short list of digital marketing agencies of no more than three as a rule of thumb, set an appointment for a consultation. It's as simple as that.

6. WHAT KIND OF CONSULTATION TO ARRANGE

There are two kinds of consultations to choose from. One is the complementary consultation and the other is a fee-based consultation. Which one you choose will depend upon what you need from a consultation and what you are prepared for.

Complementary Consultations

Usually your company will arrange for a complementary consultation where the meeting lasts no longer than half an hour presuming your company knows its purpose. The more you know what you need in a DMA, the more productive the consultation will be. When you can present your company's purpose at the meeting, the DMA will know if they can adequately service your needs.

The meeting will inform both parties rather quickly whether there is a personality fit and help enlighten on the other seven criteria for selecting a digital marketing agency.

Fee-Based Consultations

If you are looking for a consultation that allows for more exploration and a deeper analysis of your site's current traffic activity, and if you want a more comprehensive recommendation for the courses of action, you should opt for the fee-based consultation. This will also allow for more time to be spent on shared ideas.

In this consultation, be prepared to answer more questions and provide information as though your company had already hired the DMA to do the actual larger project.

7. HOW TO GET THE MOST FROM A CONSULTATION – COMPLEMENTARY VS FEE-BASED

Be prepared to present your company's overarching purpose. The more in-depth you are, the better the consultation will be. As well, make sure you have expressed that purpose in a way that can be easily understood by the digital marketing agency.

Ensure that your communication of the overarching needs of the company is effective so that the DMA understands exactly what those are. Time can be wasted on the presentation if your communication is not coherent. Take the viewpoint of the DMA when you look over your notes to check for coherency.

During the consultation, listen to ideas and advice that the DMA proposes on other possible needs or goals to help your company. Take notes on these and see how you can implement these after the consultation is over. Even if that digital marketing agency is not the one you feel fits your needs the best, there may be good advice you can implement while you look for another agency. On the other hand, listening to the suggestions made by the DMA will give you a good idea if they are a good fit for your company. For example, the Actian Corporation implemented many of the ideas that Magic Logix recommended in how to best install the Marketo automated marketing tools.

Being well-prepared will give you the best use of the consultation whether it be the complementary or the fee-based consultation.

Let's have a look now at Magic Logix's system of digital marketing. We mentioned our C3-DPO marketing approach earlier and should now cover this in greater detail. C3-DPO stands for Client 3-Dimensional Plus Operation.

MAGIC LOGIX CLIENT 3-DIMENSIONAL PLUS OPERATION

Magic Logix has a standard, yet flexible, workflow developed to center around the needs of a client in a dynamic way over time. We refer to the Magic Logix workflow (see below) as the ML C3-DPO, for Magic Logix Client 3-Dimensional Plus Operation.

It was created in-house and has proven out since 1999. And it is no wonder! As part of our standard operating procedure, ML C3-DPO ensures that Magic Logix's service is consistently of the highest quality. That ensures success for the client company as well as for Magic Logix.

When ML takes on a client as a new project, the first step is to prepare a plan of action, along with a timeframe of achieving each step of the project, and getting it agreed upon by both parties. This is the

Requirement Document, which is the name of the scope document that ML uses.

There are various methods that ML uses to collect the data in a way so that it will appear correctly in the user interface of the website. This may take into consideration the history of how the client usually collects data.

ML will also conduct a competitive research to see what the competitors are doing and saying about their own products and company as well as about the client's company and products. For example, the Pepsi and Coca cola companies do this to boost their sales. This way they can discover what has been successful for other companies, as well as what has been unsuccessful. Promotion can also play against the competitive products or companies in their content as well.

Another method of collecting data is to do A/B testing. Here, ML will see which of two ads or emails, etc., with different contents do better at pulling sales. For example, an ad stating "Buy now before supplies run out" might get fewer sales that one saying "Sale ends in two days. Buy now." This is good data to have when marketing a product.

Magic Logix also uses multivariate testing to collect data; this is different than A/B testing, in that it has multiple variations. In this method, a website page is presented differently each time a visitor comes to view the page. The variations include a different placement of the elements on the page, a different color background, a different colored button, different headlines or a different image, etc. All variations are tested to determine the viewer's response and the conversion rate. A successful digital marketer knows that how the page is balanced makes a huge difference to how viewers respond to a call to action. Using these tests help define just which variation of web page will get the right response for a sale.

Conjoint analysis is another useful tool that ML uses to find out what features in a product is more desirable to the market. The answers given to a set of survey questions enables ML to propose promotional ideas that reflect these desired features.

Lastly, there is always the qualitative feedback from the client via ML reports, calls, emails and meetings that is ever so important. Communication is vital in such an endeavor and cannot be undervalued.

At each stage of development, one of ML's senior management will review the progress through weekly reports and ad hoc to ensure the coding approach is consistent for the web as well as to do performance testing of the website. This would include how fast the website loads as well as making sure there are breaks in the links and that certain functions work properly. These are important especially for larger companies since even a few hours of something not working properly can cost them a lot of lost revenue. Doing these actions regularly has resulted in ML having consistent, timely and effective top level quality assurance.

ML PROCESS MILESTONES

| Research and Plan Strategy (1) | Setup Developing Environment (3) | Inside Template Implementation (5) | Data Migration (7) | Final Q&A and Website Launch (9) |
| Design Strategy (2) | Homepage Template Conversion & Homepage Animation (4) | Functionality Development & Third Party Integration (6) | Beta Site Launch (8) | |

THE REQUIREMENT DOCUMENT, THE SCOPE DOCUMENT USED BY MAGIC LOGIX

A scope document is a written agreement between the DMA and your company that spells out just what projects will be carried out, for how much payment and when. It covers everything that is agreed upon so that all parties know what the goal is, what resources are to hand and what the plan of action is to obtain those goals and in what time frame. This is determined by implementing phases I, II and III of the ML C3-DPO workflow as shown in the illustration below and by measuring the current and required resources to meet the agreed-upon goals set out by the client and Magic Logix. Measurables, which are statistics that can be measured and usually include various traffic and conversion metrics in Google analytics, are agreed upon and established during the strategic planning process, or phase IV and ultimately during phase V as an ongoing process.

PHASE I — DATA COLLECTION

First and foremost, ML collects the data from the client company in order to know how to best service the client. This is done by having the client complete a comprehensive survey

47

to determine the needs of their company, their objectives, things they like to avoid, their top competition and deadlines.

PHASE II — THE CLIENT ASSESSMENT QUESTIONNAIRE

Once the data has been collected, the next step is to find out what the client needs in digital marketing and what ML can do to fill those needs. Does the client need a website? Or is there a website already published on the Internet? Do they need greater sales? Is it marketing that is key here or do they need to set up a database? All of these factors need to be established so that the scope document can be drawn up in a way that ML knows what the client needs to be developed. The client also needs to know what they need so they can present that to ML. The Client Assessment Questionnaire will pinpoint these needs for the scope document. The team at Magic Logix works closely together to analyze the survey in order to create a Statement of Work (SOW).

PHASE III — GOALS AND RESOURCE ASSESSMENT

The Goals Assessment is then used for phase III to find out what the client's goals are. It's crucial that both parties have an agreement as to what is expected of them as it will provide a clear and concise flow of communication between them and prevent unnecessary hiccups. Part of this, by understanding the vision of the client, is to determine how long the project will take as well as what the end result will be.

A Resource Assessment is done as well, so that ML knows what resources are available to both parties. For example, ML will need to know what budget the client can afford currently for digital marketing, although this would possibly change as the marketing becomes more successful.

It is also used to find out what resources the client has

currently. Do they have a website currently and what type? What type of data base do they use? Is it an internal data base or an external one? Are they doing any special media or marketing? In their website an e-commerce one or not? All these, as well as what time frame is being considered, is important at this phase.

PHASE IV — MAGIC LOGIX 3D PLUS STRATEGIC PLANNING

Now that data has been collected and the needs and goals of the client are determined, the process evolves into phase IV, which is to draw up the strategic plan. This will be outlined in the Requirement Document as to what steps or stages will be done and when at what cost. It is important at this point that both parties understand just what is expected as this will be their official signed agreement.

PHASE V, WEEKLY REPORTS FROM ML AND INITIALED APPROVAL FROM THE CLIENT

This phase is ongoing with weekly reports from ML to let the client know what has been done. The client initials an approval to let ML know that the actions are accepted and that they can continue as planned. At this point, communication is very important. Both the client and the ML must know what the other is doing and if the marketing is successful or not. Also the ML needs to know if there are changes within the company or in the overall plan or goals set at the beginning.

Technical Creative Development

From this phase, Magic Logix goes into its technical creative development plus any implementation that is needed and this consists of three steps: Customization, Creative Tactic and Marketing Execution.

Let's take a look at each one of these in more detail.

Customization

No two websites are alike, and neither is how a client wants to present and promote their products or services. Therefore, it is necessary to customize what will need to be done in order to set up the right marketing for the individual client. ML does a total technical cross section customization for the client. This customization is determined by the Client Assessment Questionnaire from which ML obtains vital information from the client.

Such items that are customized are the database, programming to share with the user interface, user interface development, and digital marketing resources. Then ML does a streamline integration of everything across all of the many digital marketing channels. Let's take a look at each of these separately.

Customization of Databases

As far as a database goes, there is always some degree of customization that takes place. It's not that the customization happens in the database itself. There are other changes that may need to be made so that the database matches the needs and goals of the client and these changes are usually made indirectly through the use of tools. For example, the access may need to be changed or perhaps categories need to be implemented. There might also be the situation where a content-type database needs to be created. All sorts of conditions can exist whereby the database doesn't quite function the way it should for a client and will need to be customized.

For example, when we worked with Druple and we

had to create a content type for a blog or author content for magazines, there were different kinds of products needed. Each website has unique products or services and those changes that we make for them is part of the customization.

ML is experienced in working with a multitude of different kinds of databases; e-commerce, content-base database, etc., and making it work the way the client wants.

Customized Programming to Share Data with User Interface

In many cases, programming needs to be customized so that the data can be shared with the user interface. For example, a website functions in a different way on a desktop as compared to a tablet or smart phone, etc. Without the customization, the user interface will not function well on these various devices. We create apps/programs that are data driven, much like it is done in BaseCamp.com (an online project management and collaboration software package), so that the client's target audience can view the website and marketing on any of the devices.

Customized User Interface Development and Digital Marketing Resources

This customization has to do with the creation of a custom look and feel that is applied across all of the digital marketing campaign such as corporate website, landing pages, social media profiles, micro sites and mobile. The buying public associates a certain look that goes with the product they buy and it is crucial to maintain a standard look across the boards.

Streamline Integration

The streamlined integration that Magic Logix then does to distribute the client's brand across the many digital marketing channels is important to the success of the marketing campaigns themselves. A buyer recognizes the brand and is more likely to respond in a purchase.

Creative Tactic

Once the customization is done, ML draws up the overall website plan and implements its strategy. At this point it is important to match the target audience, get feedback from the client and continue iterative testing to ensure that the website is accessible in high quality to all devices and all browsers. Let's cover each of these a bit more fully.

Implementation of the Creative Strategy

ML presents the client with a highly professional product of website and marketing. The team at ML is fully qualified to implement the creative strategy needed and by gathering the 'needs and wants' data fully from the client is able to do so. The client will know that due to its high quality, the marketing will drive qualified customers to the client's website resulting in greater economic success.

Matching the Target Audience

The message that the marketing needs to send forth has to match the target audience in order for it to be effective. You can't sell diapers to a fisherman looking for new tackle. It's the same for the website. Thus, ML carefully scrutinizes just what will communicate to the desired audience and incorporates that into the website.

Client Feedback to ML

It's very important for the client to maintain communication with ML to give the necessary feedback that ML will use to evaluate the next creative steps to take with the website and marketing. This can never be under-evaluated and is done weekly through various face-to-face meetings such as through conferences, Go-to-meetings, Skype or other such platforms.

Ongoing Interactive Testing

Once the website and marketing is up and running, ML tests them repeatedly to make sure the strategy is completely and perfectly implemented, and that the website works on all browsers. ML also ensures that it works on all devices. That way someone using their iPhone or iPad will be able to view the website perfectly and employ all functions on the website.

It's also important that the client carries on their own quality assurance testing and can give their full approval for the finished product.

Digital Marketing Execution

Now that the website is up and running, the marketing needs to be executed. There are four areas that this entails and these we will cover in more detail here.

Customizing the Development

As with the website, the marketing itself will be customized. Magic Logix works with the client to develop the individualized marketing that is needed by that company in order to prosper. This means that the content of the promotional activities need to be consistent across all channels.

At this time, an editorial calendar would be developed to plan what ideas to publish within the marketing process and when the various pieces are sent out and to what social media or marketing avenues. Consistency in the delivered message is important here.

A social marketing plan is also discussed so that the client's objectives can be accomplished. Included here is a discussion on what ongoing communication would be needed from the client to achieve this endeavor. Changes within the client's company need to be taken into account. New products, new activities within the company and new activities for the customer as well, as sales events, will need to be marketed as they come up.

Search engine optimization is always included in marketing. Because the site will need to be easily found by internet searches, a search engine optimization is important. Correctly done, this will put the website within the first page that a search brings up to view. Both paid searches, such as pay-per-click and unpaid searches are planned for in the marketing discussions.

Lastly, discussion also centers around the custom look and feel that the client wants in order to match their brand and objectives. The features of the website and their functionality will also be discussed.

Training and Assisting the Client

Not only is Magic Logix interested in launching the website and marketing for their client, but they actively train and assist their clients in building, growing, and maturing through their product and service life cycles. This puts the client into the driver's seat from which they can take hold of their company's future prosperity.

Continuing the Follow-up

The needs of a client's customers are always changing and evolving. Therefore. Magic Logix will continue as agreed to follow up with advice and assistance for the client so that they can build new business centered on these changing needs.

The next step to selecting a DMA is to work with that agency to build your website and market your product. This takes us to the next chapter.

Chapter Three
WORKING WITH A DMA
FOR OPTIMUM RESULTS

Once you have chosen the best DMA for your digital marketing needs, the next step is to figure out how you will work together during the project development phase. The two most important factors in achieving optimum results are communication with the DMA during weekly meetings and the internal communication within your company between these meetings. This chapter will cover both in more detail.

Communication with the DMA

It is very important to know exactly what your DMA is doing with regards to your marketing. Remember that your primary goal—growing your business—is their goal as well, and their work should consistency reflect this. That means it should be in sync with your weekly business plans. The best way to stay apprised of the progress of your digital marketing projects is through regular meetings with the DMA.

Kickoff Meeting

The purpose of the first meeting with your DMA is to coordinate your efforts; this means making sure that you and the agency are on the same page regarding

your company's short and long term goals. This kickoff meeting will probably be quite a bit longer than subsequent regular meetings, which will run about thirty to forty-five minutes. At the kickoff, you will review the project as a whole, including a global view and milestones. The DMA will map out the tasks they are responsible for (namely, providing or obtaining content, site-mapping and branding guidelines), and give you a timeline for the completion of these tasks. You will also gain access to any software integration that is needed, as well as a database access, merchant account, payment gateway, license content, et cetera. At this time, it is vital that you fully understand what the DMA is presenting. Ask questions so that you have no doubt as to what the DMA will be doing and when. Another important thing you should do during the kickoff is to set a schedule of regular meetings with the DMA to ensure that milestones are being met in a timely fashion.

Desired Response to Invalid Suggestions

In the event that the DMA makes a suggestion that does not fit with your company's vision or goals, don't panic—it does not mean that you chose the wrong digital marketing company. On the contrary, part of what you are paying for is to hear their ideas, even if you do not accept all of them. As the expert in the digital marketing field, it is the DMA's job to make suggestions that will improve your business. It is also their job to demonstrate to you how they will do so. If an idea sounds unappealing at first, try to keep an open mind before dismissing it. And if you do decide that it is not what you want, be sure to let them know right away. Don't assume they will figure it out on their own; be respectful but direct and respectful and you will be laying the foundation for a strong relationship. Ultimately, it will still be your choice whether to accept or reject the DMA's ideas, but at least they will know where they stand and adjust their ideas accordingly.

Regular Meetings

How often you meet with your DMA depends on a variety of factors, including the scope of the project, client location and differences in time zone. Whatever you decide, a schedule of regular meetings should be outlined and communicated at the beginning of each project and strictly adhered to.

The regular meetings provide an opportunity for the main point of contact on the client side to dialogue with the DMA's project manager. As quality communication between the two is critical, these meetings should foster an environment of openness, where each is comfortable asking questions and providing them with honest feedback. If both the client and DMA are in the same area, in-person meeting are preferable. If not, there are other ways, such as GoTo Meeting, to conduct an internet meeting. Regardless of the location, the agenda of each meeting should correspond with the schedule laid out of the beginning of the project; it should include a discussion of the tasks that have been completed by the DMA and any client feedback or questions regarding those tasks; it should also cover the tasks that remain to complete the project any clarification that's needed to move on to the next milestone.

The lines of communication should also be kept open between meetings. For example, if the project requirements dictate monthly meetings, then there should be some sort of communication (via phone or email) between you and the DMA each week. They should be giving you regular status reports on the tasks laid out during the kickoff. Be sure to review these status reports carefully. Simply accepting the updates as proof that the DMA is doing something will not help you to guide the project.

You will then use these reports to guide the plan of action within the company. This means coordinating your staff to work in concert with the DMA; it also informs what they should expect from the promotional outflow generated by the digital marketing agency. If you have questions about the reports, make sure you bring them up to the agency.

Problems to avoid

A breakdown in communication is one of the most serious problems that can occur between you and your DMA; luckily, it is also one of the most easily avoidable. As discussed above, it is important to get the project off to a good start by clearly identifying goals in the kickoff meeting. But even before that occurs, the staff of the client company should have already collaborated internally in order to establish their goals. They then must clearly communicate these goals to the DMA. The regular meetings throughout the course of the project will then provide an opportunity for both the client and DMA to ask questions and get clarification on any items or tasks they are uncertain about. It is important that the DMA provides the client information in a language that they understand (i.e., the explanation of technical terms).

Another common problem you might encounter is difficulty in adhering to the project schedule. When projects are not completed on time, it is usually because the client did not provide content or feedback according to the timeline. Remember that as the client, you must also adhere to the timeline you agreed upon with the DMA. That means coming to regular meetings prepared to share data and ask the pertinent questions.

Have you ever had questions pop into your mind during the course of the week, only to forget them at the time of the meeting? Keep a notebook handy so you can jot down these questions as they come to you.

The DMA will also have questions for you during the

course of the project. When they bring an issue to your attention, listen carefully and take an honest look at the suggestions they make. Determine whether they are valid as quickly as possible and be sure to respond to their phone call or email in a timely fashion.

If you that feel the DMA's suggestions are not right for your business, don't be shy, Remember, you are the client, and while it is prudent to carefully consider the DMA's expert opinion, you are still the ultimate decision maker about how you want to present your company to the world. Let the agency know in a firm yet respectful manner that something they are doing is not working. Don't worry about offending them—as professionals, they will appreciate your guidance. On the other hand, they should be able to provide suitable evidence as to why they have made the suggestions. After all, they are being hired for their expertise and it is in their own interests to make your company a success, and presumably spread the word to your contacts as to what a great job they did for you.

The most important thing you should keep in mind during the weekly meetings is that it is better to ask questions than to operate on assumptions. Nothing wastes time more than basing activities on misunderstandings, either about what is currently being done to market your business, or what should be done moving forward. Misunderstandings can result in you working at cross-purposes with the DMA, and such uncoordinated actions can be destructive and might even set the company back financially.

Feedback

As mentioned above, it is critical that the client provide clear, concise feedback in a timely manner. Allowing an unsatisfactory course of action to continue is a waste of time and resources and can result in dire consequences for your company. The more details the client can provide, the better the DMA can deliver results that will grow the business.

Another thing that can really hinder the DMA in its work is with client indecisiveness (i.e. when the client changes the direction it wants to take). Deviations from initial scope of the project must be given the utmost consideration and communicated immediately to the DMA.

Internal Communication within Your Company

In order to give the DMA the guidance it needs, the decision makers within your company must first meet internally to discuss the direction of the project. You should also collect data from your staff about the DMA's progress. For example, people from one department may agree with the implementation of the marketing plan, while others may have suggestions for improvement. Either way, their input will help inform your meetings with the DMA and give them an idea of what actions will work best for your company in the future.

Make sure that you only give the most current and accurate data to the DMA. There is nothing worse than receiving incorrect and sloppily obtained data, only to work for hours on something that will not be beneficial to the client company. This is not only a waste of time, but can be damaging as well. Check and double check the data yourself, rather than relying on what you hear from others.

Regular Meetings with the DMA

It is important that you develop an internal protocol as to the information you will present to the DMA in each meeting. In others words, the DMA should be able expect consistency in the flow and quality of the information you provide them. This not only makes for more efficient project management, but it also contributes to a relationship built on mutual respect and trust.

This information should be based on the expectations and requirements that were outlined at the beginning of the project. Depending on the project, the information needed can include marketing goals, budgets, target market, sales, profit margin, sales cycle, IT infrastructure, past performance, and anything else pertinent to the project. Always be sure to inform your DMA immediately of any changes to the company. Time is of the essence when it comes to responding to a change. The agency might need to make their own changes in order to continue providing a valuable service. You must also inform the DMA of anything that tangentially affects your company-- and therefore their work--including new laws or other changes within the industry or geographical location.

Who Within the Client Company Should be Involved in Data Collection?

Ultimately, collecting data for the DMA is the responsibility of the department head(s) or any other decision makers in all divisions that will be effected by the agency's work. However, these people must first gather it from the people in the trenches. For example, if the work involves the redesign of an e-commerce site, the data will come from several different departments: IT will need to provide information about software integrations, server requirements, past performance, and security; Marketing will need to provide data on past product and consumer marketing, future goals, merchandising, and loyalty programs; Shipping and Logistics will need to provide information on processes, procedures, and order management; Accounting/ Billing will need to provide data regarding merchant account, payment provider, billing process and software requirements; and Advertising –

will need to provide data on budget, goals, markets, and previous years' data.

It is most efficient for the client to collect this data through internal meetings. The first meeting—similar to the kickoff with DMA—would be to determine all departments affected and identify a person from each to department, who is responsible for compiling that data. This person will then provide all of the information that is needed from their departments to the company's main point of contact. The department liaisons should meet with the point of contact regularly to ensure a collaborative effort and a unified output.

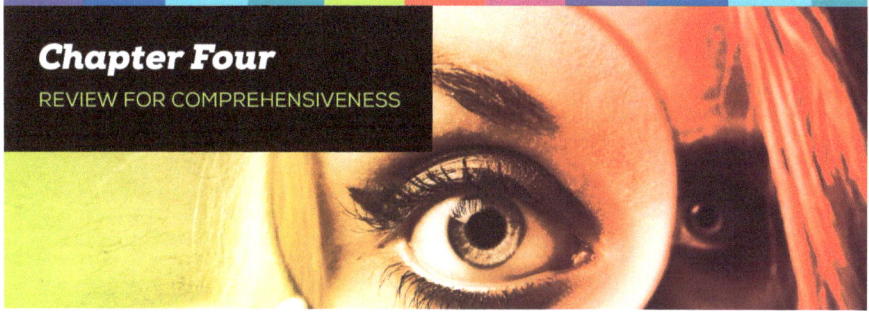

In Chapter 3, we covered how you should set up the initial processes and procedures for working with your digital marketing agency. But that is only the first step in creating a long lasting, "win-win" relationship between you and the DMA. In order to achieve and maintain the optimum marketing results, it is important that the client company take a holistic view of marketing. This chapter will focus on the benefits of such a global approach, including the use of Marketing Performance Management (MPM), to measure the success of your marketing plan and areas that need improvement.

A Holistic Approach to Marketing

Usually, when we hear the word holistic, it's in the context of healthcare. Well, the same concept applies to business. A holistic approach to marketing is good for the "health" (profitability, sustainability) of your business. The benefits of such an approach include:

- Significantly improved marketing performance through a reduction in unnecessary spending

- Superior allocation of resources

- Development and retention of customer loyalty

- Development of better programs to drive customer acquisition, revenue growth and profitability

- Optimization of the marketing mix

- Ultimately, the ability to measure and improve marketing return on investment (ROI)

The scope and breath of this approach often depends upon whether you are conducting a business-to-business (B2B) or business-to-consumer (B2C) campaign. For example, if you are marketing your product to another company, there is usually a much great sum of money at stake than if you are marketing to the individual consumer. You will also need to impress that company's management team. However, regardless of your audience or the size of the transaction, the marketing principles are the same. You must employ targeted messages and two-way engagement with that audience in order to satisfy their wants and needs more effectively. This engagement typically takes place across several channels, including advertising through search engines, banner ads, email and media-embedded placement across Web, mobile, social, TV devices and event marketing. As a result, the typical activities for optimizing the media mix, and measuring and optimizing marketing performance have become complex. Therefore, you must make sure that your DMA stays abreast of, and adapts to, emerging trends. Typically, digital marketers describe emerging technology trends in terms of channels such as smartphones, tablets or social TV. Focusing on channels alone, however, limits marketing opportunities. These trends offer opportunities to revolutionize the whole way marketing is done, including:

- Information (big data and the analytics that go with it)

- Cloud computing (campaign management software as a service)

- Real-time processes, such as pricing and targeted offers

- The "Internet of things" (pervasive connections)

Measuring the Success of a Marketing Plan

When business is good and the money is flowing in, it is easy for businesses, particularly small businesses, to become complacent in regards to their marketing plan. It is during tough economic times, however, that the importance of measuring marketing comes to light. There is an increased pressure to justify expenditures, and resulting in company execs struggling to measure the success and return on marketing investment (ROMI) of marketing programs and campaigns. Therefore, it is prudent for client-companies to measure the ROMI faithfully, from the beginning.

As you can see from the above, marketing strategies, particularly in the Technology Age, have several moving parts. In addition, these moving parts are constantly growing and evolving with the development of new technology. Take Twitter, for example, which was all but irrelevant a few short years ago but is now one of the primary avenues used to reach the consumer. As marketing plans change with the times, it is even more important for the staff of the client company to take an active role in the ongoing collection, organizing and sharing of data so they can measure the success of the current strategy. The key is to employ a system whereby the success of the marketing plan can be measured and that information can be shared—both within the company and between the company and the DMA.

One of the best ways to analyze trends in marketing is through Marketing Performance Management (MPM). MPM encompasses the technologies and services that facilitate the ability to access insights, analyze data, make predictions, and optimize marketing programs, campaigns and resources. At the foundational level, MPM includes a data repository,

BI tools and analytical workbenches. At the strategic level, MPM provides role-based access to information and KPIs through dashboards, visualization, point-and-click analysis, modeling, simulation and optimization.

MPM is a critical element of an integrated marketing management (IMM) platform, providing visibility into performance, an understanding of that performance and the ability to take action based on that knowledge. MPM also enables enterprises to make predictions about customers, markets and competitors, as well as to run simulations on future marketing scenarios and scenario planning.

The mining of data for MPM can be difficult, particularly for the aspects of marketing that are not automated, or where information is maintained by third parties such as agencies or marketing service providers. Cost data for ROMI analysis can also be difficult to collect if the company has not implemented an MRM solution for financial management. Some measures of effectiveness have required advanced modeling and attribution of revenue to different channels or marketing steps. Some marketing programs and campaigns provide only softer benefits, such as raising brand awareness or increasing customer satisfaction and loyalty.

Marketing vendors have been slow to include more-advanced capabilities in their offerings. Although more vendors are providing preconfigured dashboards and KPIs, few offer a comprehensive MPM solution with simulation and optimization models. Moreover, most vendors are still tactically focused on providing insights into the use of the software application, rather than the functional performance of the marketing organization and its processes. System integrators, professional service providers, marketing service providers and agencies are also showing interest in partnering with technology providers to build solutions around MPM, or in enhancing their consulting offerings to focus on key MPM objectives. There is also a growing market for specialty vendors focused solely on MPM. Many of the smaller, niche vendors in the market have a strong wrapper of professional services around their software solutions.

According to current assessments of business intelligence (BI), most notably, data management technologies and emerging trends, there are strong expectations from end users regarding the potential transformational value of MPM in regards to marketing efforts. Vendors are making slow, but steady progress on solutions.

What Can a Company Do to Create Holistic Marketing Strategy?

It is critical for a company's marketing department to access and measure all types of marketing programs and campaigns so that they can better allocate the appropriate resources. This responsibility ultimately lies with the senior marketing leaders or chief marketing officers (CMOs), who are under pressure from their chief financial officer (CFO) to manage costs. The CFO is of course under pressure from the CEO to drive growth. In recent years, the role of the CMO has drastically shifted toward one of more accountability for marketing performance, thus fueling interest in MPM and, ultimately, the ability to calculate a ROMI.

That said, we advise our clients to invest in MPM before it becomes mandated by the CFO; this will eliminate the need to go back over data later on. It's therefore important to consider the long-term vision of technology vendors and service providers before hiring them. The vendor you choose for IMM should have a comprehensive vision that includes MPM. Look for tools and solutions that are user-friendly and include best practices for role-based dashboards, KPIs, multidimensional analysis, visualization, point-and-click analysis and easy data navigation. You should expect some significant customization and investment in professional services, as well as software, in order to adequately measure marketing performance. Third-party vendors may also be required for advanced capabilities around marketing mix optimization. Client companies must determine where to source required data, integrate with MRM solutions to understand program and campaign costs, and plan to integrate these solutions with BI and corporate performance management (CPM) tools, leveraging standard solutions whenever possible. Ideally, the CFO should be involved with these efforts, and the MPM should be aligned with CPM.

With the proliferation of marketing applications and spreadsheets, data becomes unnecessarily siloed and harder to analyze across functional roles built around separate marketing applications. The use of siloed information becomes relegated to improving the ROI of that particular application and the specific process it automates, rather than improving the overall performance of marketing. That's why employing a system that organizes this data across all areas is critical the long term success of your marketing plan.

Historically, marketing has not been measured very well, if at all, in many areas. If this is the case with your company, MPM capabilities can be truly revolutionize your business. The ability to measure, manage and optimize will not only make marketing accountable, it will help transform it to a profit center where ROMI can be measured. Once decision-makers are aware of the costs versus expected revenue and attribution analysis, they can then make strategic decisions regarding marketing programs.

Chapter Five
A/B TESTING ONLINE

The last chapter covered the importance of taking a holistic approach to marketing, particularly in regards to the mining, analyzing and sharing of information for the purposes of measuring performance. This chapter will cover one of the methods companies can use to assess consumers' reaction to their website and other digital marketing tools. A/B testing online is a technology-aided process that optimizes online experiences by delivering various versions to an audience, then assessing which works best. As in any scientific experiment, the process tests an alternative version against a "control" (or, in the case of multivariate testing, several variations simultaneously). These tests may be targeted as well; this allows a unique audience segment to receive a different "test recipe." The important thing to remember is that online A/B testing leads to better online experiences, which in turn deliver better business metrics.

You start with an issue--let's say that you've been carefully measuring the success of your website in bringing in viable leads. Perhaps your Home page isn't as attractive as that of your

competitors; perhaps the copy doesn't properly showcase your products or there are too many questions on the form that potential consumers have to fill out to request information from you. Once you've identified the issue, the next step is to discuss how you can fix it. This is the time for you to delve into the mind of the person you want to attract to your website. If you were a consumer (or potential consumer) of your company's product and--assuming the presumed issue with the website is actually a deterrent to your purchasing it—what would fix this issue for you? This proposed solution is what you will use to form the "hypothesis", or premise you will test. Brainstorming can begin within the company, but if you are working with a marketing agency, you should bring them in as soon as possible so they can advise you about the logistics of implementing your ideas. This includes things like controlling variables that may influence the results (i.e. running a promotional sale at the same time you are making the changes to your website. How will you know which increased your website traffic?) Once these details are ironed out, you are ready to begin the A/B testing, followed up of course by measuring the results and mapping out the next steps.

The most important thing to keep in mind is that A/B testing is always a successful experiment. Even if the proposed alternate version does not increase your leads, this "failed" test has taught you what doesn't work, which is very valuable information! You can now move on to test other ideas. This is called "sequential testing", and you and your marketing agency can use it to learn what fixes will really increase your business. It can also help you identify other issues to be corrected. Sequential testing can be particularly useful to small businesses with smaller marketing budgets.

As with every other aspect of your marketing, it is important when engaging in A/B testing that there is clear understanding within the company and between the company and your marketing agency.

The Evolving Role of A/B Testing in Digital Marketing

A/B testing is not in and of itself new to marketers; in fact, it has been used for decades to gauge audiences' reaction to different variations of a product or marketing strategy. For example, it is commonly used to test a marketing tool's "call to action", or the incentive to buy. During A/B testing, groups of potential consumers are sent different version of a marketing tool (i.e., a flyer or coupon) and the one that has more success in motivating potential consumers is used in the actual campaign. The application of A/B testing to online experiences, on the other hand, is still a fairly new market. Marketing companies did attempt to utilize it in the past, but the method had been the subject of much hype and, inevitably, some disillusionment.

Nowadays, A/B's position on the Digital Marketing Cycle indicates that it is starting to be put to effective use. Yet the market for online A/B testing is still in its adolescence, largely because the workflow process for designing, implementing, executing and analyzing tests in large volumes is lacking or missing altogether. Marketing organizations that do a lot of testing use such tools as Microsoft Excel and SharePoint, or project management tools, such as Jira. Those in the high-tech, retail and media sectors are the most aggressive adopters of online A/B testing technology. Digital measurement agencies such as Brooks Bell, Stratigent, Cardinal Path and Keystone Solutions offer outsourced resources for this technology, but most do not offer creative development.

There are multiple aspects to this market. Many Web Content Management (WCM) systems, recommendation engines and targeted email campaign systems have A/B capabilities, but these are limited to the experiences delivered by those systems. General-purpose online A/B testing products, which are designed to reduce or eliminate

dependencies on IT resources or processes surrounding WCM systems, are a more interesting option for marketers.
The most common architecture for such general-purpose offerings utilizes the cloud; this enables marketers to upload content, configure, execute tests and analyze the results for themselves.

Not surprisingly, the general-purpose online A/B testing market is largely aligned with the Web analytics market. As such, many digital marketing giants now have offerings that facilitate the use of A/B testing, as this makes them more appealing to businesses of any size. Adobe, IBM, Webtrends and Google all offer tools that integrate with their own data collection, segmentation and reporting systems. Optimizely and Wingify (with its Visual Website Optimizer) are extending the market with lower-cost tools. Montetate's offering is priced somewhere in the middle and offers optional recommendation engine features. HP acquired the Optimost testing product with its purchase of Autonomy. SiteSpect has a unique offering that uses an on-premises network device to perform the tests. Other providers include Accenture (with its Digital Optimization offerings), Maxymiser and Vertster.

Issues to Consider:

Testing interactive experiences will arguably help any organization, but that does not mean it is aligned with your marketing strategy. There are several potentially prohibitive issues, such as: cost, the cultural acceptance (or lack thereof) of content stakeholders, and the complexities inherent in testing. While these factors are becoming less relevant with the arrival of lower-cost providers, easier-to-use products and more technically savvy digital marketers, there are still several moving parts involved with experiential testing. Most notably, these number of experts needed over course of the test life cycle, including feature developers, campaign developers, business managers, analysts and marketing operations staff.

Remember that before you invest your company's resources, you must be sure you are going to get a return that justifies that investment. (This builds on what we discussed in Chapter 4 about marketing measurability). In order to determine whether this kind of testing is right for your business, we recommended assigning dedicated testing engineers and, if necessary, assessing the decision-making culture. If choices are being based on "gut feelings", you may need to make changes so that those responsible for marketing strategies embrace testing as a means of collecting measurable data. On the flip side, A/B testing can make the management of your marketing more efficient. Meetings to decide content, navigation or functions become more productive. When conflicting opinions arise, you can simply decide to test the point in question and proceed to the next topic on the agenda, rather than listen to people's speculations about what might work best.

When starting out with online A/B testing, tackle the "low-hanging fruit"; this generally provides a good return on investment (gains of 10% or far more are common). Once a testing program is well under way, the gains may moderate, but can still be significant. Many organizations run multiple tests concurrently, with each test lasting weeks, and some run thousands of tests each year. You should bear in mind, however, that testing on this scale does not work well unless properly managed.

When employing online A/B testing, we also recommend the following:

- Align tests with audience segments; running a single test for the whole audience is not the best option. User experience and business results may vary by factors such as gender, age, location, date and time, access device and customer value.

- Use a "ready, fire, aim" approach. If your online presence is not well monetized, you can still benefit by experimenting with lower-cost online A/B testing tools to learn their benefits and procedural requirements. Start with Web testing, and then move on to digital marketing campaigns, such as those using email and display advertisements.

- Seek help from interactive agencies if time or resources are in short supply or if your organization is weak at the creative side of test development.

- Share the insights you gain from testing with your application and content developers, and encourage them to design with testing methodology in mind.

Ultimately, you must remember that A/B testing is nothing to be afraid of. Some people, for example, focus too much on ROI when developing a hypothesis. Marketing experts will advise against this, as it will skew the test results, particularly if you are afraid of your boss's reaction. Rather than worrying about a failed test, think of it as a learning experience that will further inform your marketing plan.

Marketing techniques have always been inexorably intertwined with technology; therefore, advancements or trends in one deeply impact the other. Consider Twitter, for example. Not all that long ago, Twitter was just another way to connect with friends; essentially, it was a glorified text message. Now it is arguably the most important marketing tool out there, with companies of all sizes—including Starbucks--jumping on the bandwagon. Anyone who has been to Starbucks knows how long the lines are. To remedy this situation, the coffee giant now invites people to tweet their order so it is ready by the time they arrive. In this way, Twitter is more than a simple marketing tool; it has literally become a service Starbucks offers to make itself more appealing to busy consumers. Similarly, any company seeking to either reach new markets or grow their business within a given market must stay abreast—even ahead—of new marketing trends and be ready to implement them.

That said, we advise companies to hire one agency that provides a full menu of services (i.e. web design and development, social media marketing,

search engine marketing and marketing automation), rather than a bunch of smaller, specialized agencies. This "one-stop shopping" approach makes it easier to create a seamless marketing plan. It also facilitates communication, both within your company and between the company and the DMA, which, as we discussed in earlier chapters, is a critical aspect of marketing success. Working with different agencies adds several layers of bureaucracy, for you are now trying to coordinate efforts between these agencies, as well as within different departments of your own company. This creates greater chances for miscommunication, including the possibility of people working redundantly or at cross-purposes.

If you already have a strong relationship with a small, specialized marketing company, it may be difficult to cut ties; however, you must seriously consider whether their inability to provide all the services you need will hinder your marketing plan. That said, whether you have hired that one company or are still working with multiple vendors, we make the following recommendations on how to use marketing to grow and build your company.

Since we're discussing the world of e-commerce, it would best to start with a breakdown of what makes a successful e-commerce site and the best tools to manage it as part of your comprehensive marketing plan.

E-commerce

E-commerce—or the buying and selling of products and services over the World Wide Web—is another area that has grown in leaps and bounds, particularly since people no longer have to be sitting at their computer to buy something. They now make purchases on the go, using their smartphones and tablets to access commerce sites (which are just websites that allow purchases). The strength of a web store is its ability to capitalize on uniquely digital assets such as:

- Infinite Inventory, pulling information or inventory from any node within the network.

- Social Shopping via Wisdom of Crowds and powered by Reviews and Social Networks.

- Flexibility and an ability to create a one-to-many, one-to-some or one-to-one shopping experiences based on patterns or real time behaviors.

The 12 E-commerce Components

Typical components of an e-commerce store are:

- Home Page – sets the tone and tells the consumer "who are we" and "what we are all about".

- Images – pictures and graphics that speak to brand and shopper aspirations.

- Copy – clever, pithy words that speak to brand and shopper aspirations.

- Navigation (or "menu" or taxonomy) – provides shopping paths. For example, if you are shopping at Target online, you can click on "Home Goods", "Electronics", et cetera.

- Categories – groups of products to aid in merchandising, shopping and SEO. For example, types of women's clothing—skirts, coats, et cetera.

- Product Pages – this is where the magical BUY button lives, along with a product's story, reviews and specifications or features.

- Shopping Cart – where shoppers "put" their products while browsing, then use during checkout.

- Content Pages – "About us", "Contact us", guarantee and a return policy are typical e-commerce content.

- Site Search – this is an "internal search" of a website's content, as opposed to an "external search" on the web.

- Forms – When you subscribe to a site's email list, you use a web form.
- Metadata – feeds keywords to search engines to help index a site.
- Analytics – codes feeding usage data to programs, such as Google Analytics. Google Analytics reports data like how many new and repeat visitors your site is getting. It also reports on "bounce rate", which is how long a visitor stays on your site before "bouncing off" to another. Whether your site's bounce rate is good or bad often depends upon what kind of site you have.

Once a website has all these components, the Internet Masters, Web Masters and Web Merchandisers must have a platform that ties them all together into an efficient, easily understandable system. These platforms are called Content Management Systems, and they enable businesses to organize, merchandise, modify and create their stores.

In the "old days", companies needed Information Technology pros to do something as simple as change a product's color variation or add a new product. Thankfully, that's not the case anymore, but not all Content Management Systems were created equal, and they are not all appropriate for every application. At Magic Logix, we mainly use Magento platform to develop e-commerce sites for our clients. Magento is a powerful and flexible CMS, and we have found that it facilitates our work and suits most client company's needs.

Responsive Web Design

World Wide Consortium (W3C)

As with any other industry, there are standards to that guide website developers, designers, and online marketers; these standards, which is collectively known as the World Wide Consortium (W3C) are designed to ensure things like easy navigation, fast loading time, and accessibility for all viewers, including those with disabilities. It is also the standard for SEO and the indexing of each page of the site. W3C encompasses an enormous body of information and includes large in-depth, technical standard for Web design, Web applications, Graphics, HTML & CSS, Internalizations, Accessibility, Audio and Video Standards, Browsers and Authoring Tools, Semantic Web, Web Architecture, XML Technology, and so on. When vetting a web design company, you can check out the W3C Website Validation Service, W3C CSS Validation Service, and WDG HTML Validator—they all list website errors. The goal of the W3C is also to ensure that websites are accessible across all devices, including mobile devices, smart phones, interactive television systems, kiosks, and voice response systems, which, as we mentioned above is critical in today's marketing paradigm. The W3C provides several benefits for website owners and users alike.

Benefits for the Website Owner

- Lower Cost of Production – the standard means quicker production time and dramatically lower costs for Bandwidth and Hosting.

- Preventative Future Maintenance – with uniform development and maintenance standards, it makes it easy for other developers to understand programming code for changes in development, styling, or layout.

- Competitive Advantage – complying with these standards gives you an advantage over competitors, including faster speed, and better functionality and security for your consumers.

- Easier for Developers – these standards make it easier for any experienced developer to make changes to the code.

- SEO Friendly

- Long-Term Viability – You are ensured a long-term viability of any web document or application.

- Accessibility – Federal and State Government sites require the website to meet W3C standards in order to be Section 508 compliant.

- Privacy and Security – Building your website on a secure framework, for example, using an XML signature, encryption, and xkms, puts your consumers' minds at east.

- Increased Potential Market Share – Increased viewers may result in higher conversion and more referrals.

- Public Relations – when your site adheres to this standard, you are establishing a reputation for quality and reliability.

- For Online Merchants/E-commerce Websites – Customers are more likely to utilize your website if your online shopping carts are accessible on a secure, trustworthy shopping interface.

Benefits for the Website Viewer (Your Targeted Audience)

- Improves the User Experience – This means that pages load quicker, which decreases user frustration and the likelihood that they will leave your site.

- Increased Accessibility for All – This makes it possible for users with disabilities (whether blind or vision impaired, dyslexic, or motor skill impaired) to access your site's content. It does this by utilizing screen readers, browsers, text based browsers, hand-helds, search robots, printers, et cetera.

- Viewable to Wide Range of Devices – This allows users to access the site via their mobile devices (iPod Touch, iPad, Smart Phones, et cetera) as well as their computers.

- Print Friendly – It also provides print friendly versions for all website pages.

Social Media

These days, every business, regardless of its size or type, needs a social media strategy. If your company is very large, you might already have social media experts on staff. However, if you are a small to mid-size company looking to grow and build, it's time to consider hiring a social media company to lay out and implement a sophisticated marketing plan. Outsourcing your marketing demands allows you to expand your social media presence without increasing overhead by employing new staff or renting larger premises.

As we said above, these days you are not just targeting the PC or MAC user; most people use their smartphones for social media as well. This makes having a presence on Facebook, Twitter, and other social media sites an imperative. The question is, how do you know who your target audience is, and how do you make sure that you are not spending your time—not to mention your budget--aiming your media at the wrong people?

This is where the expertise of a social media company comes in. When vetting potential agencies, make sure specialize in influencer marketing and online influence. Influencer marketing is directed not at the ultimate consumer, but those who influence the consumer, such as celebrities, journalists, organizations, et cetera. This is not a new marketing concept, but has been adapted to digital age marketing. Marketing experts will ensure that your content is being viewed by the correct audience and they will assist you in updating your content so that it is always current.

A professional company will also be able to see the next big trend and help your company get in on the ground floor. For example, Instagram—a social media site focusing on photos and videos, is the latest craze in social media marketing. Several Fortune 500 companies—Nike, Ralph Lauren and Whole foods, to name a few--are actively marketing through Instagram. Recent studies show that Instagram can help companies of any size, including start-ups. Marketing experts can advise on whether you should focus on videos or photos, as well as the best times to post, based on your target audience.

Depending on the social media sites you choose to work with, you can share your pages as well as upload photos, videos and much more. These points are important within your strategy, and it will be the job of your social media company to manage them. By correctly implementing the best social media strategy for your business, your social media company will help you generate traffic to your content, without wasting your human and/or financial resources.

Implementing Your Social Media Strategy

The Internet is a vast, sometimes intimidating world; that's why it's so advantageous to hire a social media company to navigate this world for you. Some companies hesitate to spend the money; however, hiring a social media company actually saves you money in the long run. It is less expensive than hiring a full-time staff person or team to handle your marketing, thereby cutting your costs while increasing your top line. It's a win-win situation for any business.

Engaging professionals also minimizes the time wasted on efforts that hit the wrong audience. What's more, once you know that your social media strategy is in safe hands, you can really concentrate on the day-to-day running of your business. Even if you enjoy managing the social media yourself, the truth is that it is time-consuming. Social media sites are constantly evolving; therefore, whoever is managing the social media will have to stay on top of these changes and be able to use them efficiently. If they don't, your strategy may be obsolete before it even gets off the ground. Just adding content to your pages on a regular basis takes time and energy that can be better used in other areas of your business.

Remember that properly implementing a social media strategy takes a team of experts: content writers, graphic designers, web developers and video producers. That's why it doesn't make sense for smaller companies to have all of them on staff, particularly when they are trying to grow. Their money is better spent on hiring marketing experts like Magic Logix to manage their Facebook, Twitter and other social media campaigns.

SEO

Search engine optimization (SEO) is a strategy to promote website exposure through higher visibility in the search engines, with the ultimate goal of increasing website traffic. This can be done in one of two ways: you can do it yourself, or you can hire an SEO company to do the work for you. While the former cannot guarantee satisfactory results, the latter is a great way to drive more visitors to your site and ensure they are the right visitors for your market.

Reasons for Hiring an SEO Company

An SEO Understands Search Engine Algorithms

When you want information from the web, you go to a search engine, such as Google or Bing, and type in a term or question. Within seconds, hundreds of sites appear, ranked according to their relevance to what you typed into the search engine. It may seem like magic, but it is actually pure computer science. Behind the scenes, search engine algorithms are wading through billions of pieces of information and calculating what sites will give you what you're looking for. Well, that same algorithm is what ranks your company's website when a potential consumer does a search. An SEO company understands the nature of these search engine algorithms, which gives them the ability to strategically increase your website's ranking. Now, you could--after much studying and a thorough analysis--figure this out on your own; however, it will be a time-consuming and tedious process. The SEO people are already experts, able to easily and quickly increase your ranking. This frees you up to focus on other aspects of your business.

You Can Expect Quality Results

The people at SEO companies eat, breathe, and sleep search engine algorithms; this is their specialty. They already have processes in place, so you can expect a systematized implementation of their work. Over the course of the project, your SEO will send you regular updates and periodic reports so that you can see if they are performing as promised. Per industry standards, these reports should be both detailed and comprehensive, describing the work and any improvements in your company's search engine rankings. If they are doing their job, there will be little need for your hands-on involvement in this area.

Again, we highly recommend hiring an SEO company. When you do the SEO work on your own, you lose time and potential revenue while you learn metrics, benchmarks and other tools to make the work more effective and efficient.

As you being the hiring process, remember to exercise due diligence. There are many SEO companies claiming to be experts, so be sure to find a credible and legitimate company that already has demonstrable experience in the field. Be cautious of companies who have just entered into the SEO business with a technical staff run by novices and amateurs, as this could cost you time and resources without delivering the results you need.

Marketing Automation

This involves certain software platforms that perform repetitive marketing actions, thereby saving time and reducing human error. The marketing person inputs certain parameters for these actions, then the software does the rest. A good platform streamlines process, generates more viable leads, and improves overall marketing efficiency. Two such companies are Marketo and Eloqua Corp.; both save time and money and expedite growth for large and small companies alike.

When choosing a marketing agency, you want to be sure that they will provide you with a well-rounded selection of services. They should offer diverse options that fit the size of your company and meet your budget and goals. Marketing automation will complement the agency's other services and optimize the results of your overall marketing campaign, by:

- Improving existing digital marketing services – By moving beyond the email blast to lead nurturing programs powered by marketing automation, you can make social media a part of every campaign and deliver the content buyers want, when they want it.

- Maximizing website launch results – Leads from a newly launched website must be properly nurtured; otherwise, they can wither on the vine, making the website appear ineffective at delivering sales-qualified leads. Marketing automation helps you maximize a website launch effort by progressing leads through the buyer funnel, so more leads convert to sales opportunities.

- Optimizing outsourced sales programs – They increase effectiveness of outsourced sales resources by focusing their time on sales-ready leads nurtured with relevant content and prioritized with custom lead scoring.

The following are specific examples of what some marketing companies offer around a marketing automation platform:

- A business process/discovery workshop to learn more about your business

- A dedicated account manager

- Website and Salesforce integration

- Availability of best practices and resources

- ROI analysis on an ongoing basis

Here are some sample packages offered by Magic Logix:

Sample Package 1: Basic Tune-up:

This package is perfect for a small team of marketers with limited resources who want to improve their ability to deliver sales-qualified leads. The buyer of this package already has a broad assortment of content that can be organized to cover each stage in the buying cycle and has a good sense of what his or her goals are for the marketing program. A similar service could be offered to a more established marketing organization that already has a marketing automation platform in-house.

Services Offered:

- Basic batch Email marketing creation and deployment
- Real-time triggered email monitoring
- Basic lead storing setup
- Online behavior monitoring
- Landing page development
- Basic form development
- X consulting hours to be used anytime

Sample Package 2: Intermediate Management

This package is perfect for a company that needs extra help with an existing campaign development and management program. It is designed for companies looking to enhance their current team with expert knowledge and resources.

Services Offered:

- Everything that is offered in Package 1
- Customized email and landing page templates
- Program management

- Event marketing program creation
- Lead nurture track creation
- Regular A/B testing
- Sales alerts, email creation, and intelligence
- Segmentation best practices
- Content marketing strategy and content creation: X amount
- of content pieces per contract
- X amount of monthly hours for services
- Bi-monthly reviews

Sample Package 3: Full Managed Services

This package is designed for companies that have the resources to bring marketing automation in-house, but have chosen instead to fully outsource a managed service solution.

Services Offered:

- Everything that is offered in Package 2
- Full implementation roadmap and blueprint
- Maturity roadmap creation
- Full technical setup
- Sales and marketing alignment process development
- Lead lifecycle blueprint
- Social media campaign creation and management
- Website optimization
- Data cleanup
- List segmentation and analysis

- Buyer persona development
- Content marketing strategy and content creation: X amount of content pieces per contract
- X amount of monthly hours for services
- Bi-monthly reviews

Sample Package 4: Full Service—Client-owned Marketing Automation

This is a package specifically for companies who have already implemented marketing automation, but might not be realizing full ROI potential or who need some assistance to get it off the ground.

Services Offered:

- Expert health check into your existing instance
- Data cleanup
- Salesforce re-integration
- Campaign building
- Lead nurture track development
- Lead scoring setup
- SEO services
- Buyer persona development
- Content marketing strategy and content creation: X amount of content pieces per contract
- Maturity roadmap creation
- Social media campaign development and management
- X amount of monthly hours for services
- Bi-monthly reviews

The Role of Big Data

There are billions of piece of information floating around on the Internet—not just in the form of articles, videos, et cetera, but information on the users themselves. Big Data marketing—essentially the strategic mining, management and analysis of this information--has become a colossal industry. Experts in this field can go through that data to help you find the gems (info on potential customers) to grow and build your business.

How does a marketing company help you utilize Big Data? They have the time, the expertise and the technological capabilities to cull through this information and help you create targeted strategies for growth. This information can be used via your CMO, as well as your staff members (i.e. salespeople and customer service reps), to reach consumers.

When choosing a company to assist you with Big Data marketing, make sure that they have experience, particularly the ability to work with your key objectives and find information that is aligned with those objectives. Once your initial benchmarks are met, you can set new goals and start mining the data all over again.

Conclusion:

In conclusion, when you are trying to grow and build your business, it is critical to hire a full service marketing company that can offer you a plan tailored to your specific goals. That requires some vetting on your part. Marketing professionals must be able to assess three aspects of current market demand: total market demand; area market demand; and actual sales and market share. The measurement process is currently driven by online marketing database systems that are developed through dedicated market assessment organizations, as well as the actual buyers and sellers within an industry. The gathering and distribution of information is now becoming more timely and responsive due to computer networks and buyer/supplier networks in both consumer and business markets.

Just as important, the marketing agency should be able to help you forecast future demand. Market estimates are needed in order to judge future sales and marketing potential in various countries, regions, cities and towns. This will enable your organization to allocate marketing budgets more cost effectively amongst chosen locations. Finally, whoever markets your company should be able to assist you with determining what makes your business unique and capitalizing on that. It also must stay ahead of the current marketing trends.

Chapter Seven

DIGITAL MARKETING PITFALLS

Over the past six chapters, we have discussed the best practices for digitally marketing your business. We have also given our recommendations for creating your marketing plan, what to look for in a digital marketing agency, and the need to continually monitor the success of your strategy (and make adjustments accordingly). A poorly planned or executed marketing plan will not only hinder the growth of your business, it can actually harm it. Whether you are currently working with a professional agency or will do so in the future, keep in mind that it's easier to steer clear of pitfalls than to clean up the damage later. Here are some of the most common digital marketing pitfalls and advice on how to avoid them.

Failure to Properly Plan

As with any marketing strategy, it is important to carefully research and plan your digital marketing campaign. This is the all-important brainstorming phase, and it begins with the question: what is the primary goal of our marketing campaign? Well, it's probably to grow and build your company; however, you need to break it down into measurables. Once you have answered that question, then you can begin

breaking the plan down into different aspects—such as social media campaign— state specific goals for that particular and determine how it will factor into the big picture. Once that is done, the next question becomes, how will we measure performance? What tools will you need to measure it? If you have not done so already, this is the time when you should discuss whether you are going to hire a digital marketing agency to implement your strategy and help you tweak it. If you do decide to bring in the experts, they can help you determine what tools to use to measure performance, and how to integrate all the components into your overall marketing plan. You and your staff will still need to make several critical decisions, including the social media channels you want to work with (Facebook, Twitter, YouTube, a blog, et cetera), and the process for crafting and approving compelling content for your website, email blasts, and other tools. You will also need to choose the person or team of persons who will liaise with the digital marketing agency.

Heavy Reliance on Marketing Automation

Marketing Automation is an important component of a well-rounded marketing plan; however, it is not the entire plan. One of the biggest mistakes people make is assuming that marketing automation will fix the other problems in their marketing strategy. It is imperative that you have clear, compelling content, calls to action and landing pages in place before you begin marketing automation; otherwise, it will just continue sending "mistakes" to your audience. This will not help your bottom line; in fact, it is more likely to damage it.

Personalization is also a critical piece of marketing automation. Think of it not as a "one- size-fits-all approach", but a targeted strategy to give your audience a better experience. For example, email blasts will not work for everyone. Companies like Amazon and Netflix understand this—they provide website visitors with suggestions based on their previous searches and/or purchases. This approach is excellent because it does not annoy potential customers with a slew of emails; however, it does personalize and optimize their experience when they do go to your site.

This brings us to another point, namely, that you must make sure you are generating traffic to your site before beginning marketing automation. Studies show that the average email database expires at a rate of about 25% a year. That means if your database is not constantly expanding, it is constantly shrinking! Think of your marketing plan as a funnel: the top of the funnel represents website visitors; the middle represents sales leads; and the bottom represents actual customers. Your marketing automation may help you convert traffic to leads and leads to customers; however, it will not fix the fundamental problems with getting new people to visit your site.

Failure to Change with the Times

This has been a running theme throughout the book: digital marketing techniques are evolving apace with technology, and in order to successfully market your business you must stay abreast (preferably, ahead) of the trends. Take email, for example: it is no longer the primary digital marketing tool. Experts estimate that 80% of email users don't read all of their emails because they are tired of being inundated with messages from every website they visited. In fact, certain email providers have taken steps to parcel out advertising from regular messages (i.e. Gmail's new Priority Inbox), essentially saying they are one step above SPAM). A digital marketing company will be three steps ahead of the trends and help you segue from an outdated mode of advertising (such as email blasts) and into the up-and-coming (such as Instagram). Additionally, when you do use email, they will make sure the content is relevant and compelling. Remember, whereas your company's staff is juggling multiple tasks, a digital marketing company's primary job is to keep on top of these trends and make sure your company takes full advantage of them.

Mistakes in Web Design/Development

Your company's website is arguably the most important part of your marketing strategy. It is your company's "face" on the Internet, there for all the world to see. Even if you do nothing else to market your business, your website must be appealing, professional and, above all, efficient.

Here are the most common mistake companies make when designing and developing their websites and ways in which a digital marketing agency can fix them.

- No Search Box – Users must be able to type in keywords and search terms (much like when you're doing a search on Google or Bing) that will take them the information they looking for within the site.

- Poor Readability – Your website should have a clear font, used consistently throughout the site, as well as a balanced ratio of color and whitespace. HTML should be used to create content. It is also important to regularly update your content and correct it for typos and spelling errors.

- Unorganized Content Layout – Most users quickly scan a site until they find the information they are looking for. Use bullets, keywords and paragraphs to make that information easy to find.

- Poor Navigation – Statistics shows that if users cannot find what they want in 3 clicks, they will leave your website (and go to one of your competitors!). To avoid this, be sure that there are no dead links on your site; use text to describe those links (so the user knows what they are clicking on); and use text to explain any images. It is also recommended that you organize navigation around your website's theme.

- Inconsistent Interface Design – Everyone wants an eye-catching website, but is there is such a thing as being "too creative". The general rule is to use a simple template and use it consistently throughout the site. You want to be especially careful about using background music. At best, music is considered unimportant by users; at worst, it is considered annoying. If you must use music, be sure that it's playing continuously (as opposed to stopping and starting when the user clicks on a new page), and give the user the option to mute or shut off the music.

- Unfriendly Screen Resolution – In the "olden days", it was expected that you would have to scroll horizontally to see the whole screen. Today, that is no longer the case; in fact, websites that are not designed to fit any screen are considered poorly done. You can use Google Analytics or W3 Browser Stats to find the optimum resolution (currently it is 1024 x 768 pixels).

- Long Registration Forms – Users are visiting your website to learn about your business, not teach you about them. If you must have a registration form, keep it simple—name and email. Remember, you can learn about your visitors in other ways; for example, interacting with them through social media. That way, they feel like you care about their opinions, rather than just their email address.

- Over-Advertising – Other things that distract and annoy users include using too many automated images; allowing pop-ups to appear; and having too many advertisements. If your website takes too long to load (usually because of an automatic start-up video), you are guaranteed to lose visitors.

Basically, the rule of thumb is that functionality is more important that appearance. If you make sure your site is fast and user-friendly, people will want to return.

Disobeying the Rules of Search Engine Optimization (SEO)

In our earlier discussion of SEO, we stated that a thorough knowledge is critical to boosting your company's website ranking on search engine like Google or Bing. With enough time and patience, your company's staff can learn the complexities of SEO; however, during that time you might be losing your competitive edge, potential customers and, ultimately, revenue. A digital marketing agency already knows the ins and outs of SEO and can therefore help you avoid these common pitfalls:

- Website Functionality – This refers to the navigation issues mentioned above, such as dead links or invalid site maps.

- Linking to "Bad Neighborhoods" – Be sure that your site does not link to other sites with bad SEO practices or are otherwise untrustworthy.

- Lack of 301 Redirect – A 301 redirect signifies that the site the user is requesting has been permanently moved, then sends that user (and search engines) to a different URL. Not having a 301 redirect negatively affects your ranking.

- Excessive Use of Keywords – Keywords are an important part of your site's searchability; however, when you use too many of these keywords, your site can be labeled as SPAM. Related to this is "Keyword Stuffing", which is when the content appears to be created solely for the purposes of the search engines.

- Hidden Links – These are links that are the same color as the background of the page and therefore not visible to the human eye.

- Duplicate Pages – It is important to keep each page of your site fresh and original. Search engines disfavor sites that only slightly vary content from page to page.

- Lack of Unique Title and Meta Tags – Each page should have a unique title and meta descriptions.

- "Dynamic" URL – This is one of those times when it does not pay to be too creative. Be sure your URL has keywords that are related to the page.

- Using Pictures for Navigation – Search engines tend to favor text over images, as text has stronger algorithms (and is therefore more easily tracked for data collection).

Spreading Yourself Too Thin

This is a strong temptation for many companies, especially when it comes to social media. There are many venues, and they are all open for business, twenty-four hours a day, seven days a week. Your first instinct may be to tweet and post on Facebook several times a day, about anything even remotely related to your business. It is important to pull back and carefully consider what will be serve your target market and encourage them to do business with you. Make sure your messages are concise, based on market research and aimed at your target audience. Also, be sure to pace your posts; you want people to look forward to them.

Another temptation is to create profiles across several channels, but remember: just because your profiles are free to create does not mean the social media campaign won't cost you anything. Someone—whether it's you, your staff, or your marketing agency—will be spending a lot of time maintaining these accounts. If you are just beginning your social media marketing campaign, start small. Focus on creating quality copy, videos, pictures, et cetera for Facebook and Twitter, rather than trying to maintain several channels at once. Once you perfect these efforts, you can expand your campaign.

Treat Your Marketing Campaign as a Marathon, Not a Sprint

There is little doubt that this is the era of instant gratification, and the Internet has a lot to do with that. These days, we expect everything to appear magically at our fingertips, as quickly as a Google search. But there are still things that take time to cultivate, and that includes your social media marketing efforts. While it is true that your carefully planned strategy can bring fast results, it is important to remember that the real, sustainable growth comes over time. You must build an online presence, which will continue to evolve along with the changing technology. For example, when you begin your strategy, Facebook may bring the greatest results; a few months later, you may find that Twitter or even Instagram is the best place for your efforts. Also remember that social media requires a long-term, time-consuming commitment. You must continually update your content aimed at your target audience, in a targeted fashion (i.e. you want to tweet and post to Facebook enough to maintain a presence but not so much that people will ignore your posts or worse, become annoyed). You have to find that middle ground that keeps your friends and followers engaged and looking forward to your next update.

It's Not Enough to Create the Profile

Creating that Facebook page is just the beginning. In order to get friends and followers, you must "court" your target audience. What you use to entice them will depend on the nature of that audience; however, it should always be aligned with your other marketing strategies. If you plan properly and execute diligently, your audience will soon come to you.

Don't Be One of the Crowd

Internet users are overloaded with information every time they log on; therefore, it is becoming more difficult—and more important—to distinguish your company from the competition. Every business is unique, so find out what makes your company special and capitalize on that. We are not suggesting you reinvent the wheel when it comes to marketing methods; we're just reminding you that there is no one-size-fits all strategy. As with all marketing plans, a successful social media strategy begins with a true understanding of your consumers and their particular needs.

Mind Your Manners

Remember that social media is all about building and maintaining relationships. So while it's productive (and expected) to offer special deals for those who "friend" or "follow" your company, it's not good to do so continually. You don't want to be considered the Twitter equivalent of SPAM. Also, remember to engage your customers. Ask for their feedback about your product, including what they think you can do better. Today's consumers, particularly those who utilize social media, want to feel like you value their opinion as well as their business.

Don't Procrastinate

Let's face it: given today's business climate, your social media strategy should already be well underway. If it's not, developing and implementing it should be number one on your priority list. No matter what industry you are in, chances are that thousands, if not millions of people, are discussing its products or service online. It is imperative that you become part of that conversation as soon as possible. It will allow you to build your brand, attract new customers, and keep existing ones.

Don't be Pennywise and Pound Foolish

Social media has long been considered the purview of the young—those who came of age texting and tweeting and posting. That said, it is often tempting for smaller companies to delegate the management of their social media to an intern. Don't do this! Remember that underlying every digital marketing strategy are traditional, tried and true marketing principles. Just because someone is under 25 and has 800 Facebook friends does not mean he/she is understands these principles, knows how to engage your target audience or write compelling copy. If they do not handle your online presence in the right way, they can cause your business severe—perhaps even irreparable--damage. We've all heard of the public outrage sparked by the offensive tweet or Facebook post of a celebrity or politicians. You would rather be spending time and money on promoting your business, rather than defending it. Here is a helpful tip in choosing the staff to manage your social media—ask yourself whether you would have this person attend a high-level conference. Your marketing plan is just as important.

Another temptation for businesses with small budgets is to go with independent SEO "salespersons" or "consultants". They tend to promise the moon and the stars but deliver very little. Make sure person you're talking to can show you quantifiable results for specific clients; if they can't, you'll need to choose someone else.

These guidelines are important whether you are at the beginning of your marketing campaign or overseeing the work of the digital marketing agency. If you keep them in mind, your consumers will come to know you as the reliable, trustworthy and diligent company you are!

AB testing – used to determine the better of two variations of the same thing; a methodology in advertising where randomized experiments are utilized with two variants—A and B—which are the control and treatment in a controlled experiment.

Actian – a global corporation that mines and analyzes Big Data to gives its clients the competitive advantage. Actian has worked with such industry giants as eBay and Office. Headquartered in California, it has offices in Austin, New York, London, Paris, Frankfurt, Amsterdam, New Delhi and Melbourne.

AGILE – a method of project management typically used in software development. Using this method, teams can respond positively to unpredictable circumstances.

AJAX – a technique employed by web developers to produce interactive web applications. Dynamic websites, like those coded using AJAX, allow for a wide range of user interactivity.

Analytics – "Analytics are numbers that provide an objective measure of activities that move your business towards your business goals.

B2B – Business-to-Business

B2C – Business-to-Consumer

Blog (short for "web log") – a type of website used to publish information and personal thoughts. It is a platform for the blog's owner to voice his/her opinion on any topic, including health, spirituality, politics, and of course—commerce. Like any website, a blog's goal is to get traffic; the owner is trying to engage his/her reader, which they can do by leaving comments and "following" the blog. Blogs are commonly used as a marketing tool (for example, the blog on a business website will have posts of interest to their target consumer).

Brand – A corporate identity; it encompasses the name, slogan, logo, or anything else that distinguishes it from other companies.

Brand Character – a person, animal or some other entity that becomes synonymous with a company's brand, such as Ronald McDonald or M&Ms. A successful brand character is one that consumers can connect with on a personal level.

Campaign – a specific, defined, carefully researched series of activities used to promote a person or product. To be successful, one must know their place in the market.

Campaign Monitoring System – a software platform that delivers analytics on the marketing campaign. An efficient monitor will collect information on you is responding the campaign (clicking and forwarding links, liking them on Facebook, mentioning it on Twitter, et cetera).

CMO – the corporate executive responsible for company's marketing activities.

CMS – Content Management System: this system is a computer program operated from a central interface that allows for publishing, editing and modifying content. It is used by internet users to create websites online and can be a simple system with a few features or a more complex system with a lot more involved functions.

Competitive Research – research to find out what your competitors are doing, saying, et cetera.

Conjoint Analysis – conjoint analysis is a method of using survey questions to find out how the market values each feature of your product or service. In this way, a prediction can be made of the value of any combination of these features. One can also determine how the market will react to various feature trade-offs that you might be considering. By studying the valuations made by the respondents, one can then determine the features most desired and include them in their product as well as in the promotion of the product. It can even be used to predict the profitability of new designs.

Contenders – to parties to a contest or competition

Conversion Metrics – data, such as site visitors and bounce rate, that can be turned into viable leads and/consumers.

CRM – customer relationship management tools. In marketing, it measures the success of a campaign by tracking data via email, Internet searches, website clicks, telephone calls, et cetera.

Database – a collection of data

DMA – Digital Marketing Agency

Drivers – a computer program that controls a particular type of device—such as a printer—that is attached to the computer.

Drupal – Created in 2001, Drupal is one of the original CMS systems. It is very powerful and developer-friendly, making it the system of choice for feature rich, data-intensive websites, including Whitehouse.gov and Data.gov.uk. Like WordPress and Joomla, Drupal is open-source and based on PHP.

Eloqua – a company specializing in marketing automation

Extensible Markup Languages (XML) – designed to transport and store data on the Internet. They are seen most commonly in RSS feeds. It works well in many industries and it's compatible with many platforms.

Fortune 1000 – a list of the 1000 largest American companies, as reported by Fortune magazine

FTP – the standard abbreviation for File Transfer Protocol. This is used in the computer industry to transfer files over the Internet from one hosting company to another. FTP has facilitated this once complex process.

HTML5 – a mark-up language used for structuring and presenting content for the World Wide Web and core technology of the Internet. It is the fifth revision of the HTML standard, and its goal is to provide support for the latest multimedia while keeping it easily readable by humans and consistently understood by computers and devices. It added many features, including new video, audio and canvas elements, making it easier to handle this content without having to use plugins and APIs.

Innovators – those who introduce a new idea; a change agent

Interface – In computer science, an interface is the point of interaction with software, or computer hardware, or with peripheral devices such as a computer monitor or a keyboard. Some computer interfaces such as a touchscreen can send and receive data, while others such as a mouse or microphone, can only send data.

Iterative Testing – testing that is repeated numerous times during the development phase (i.e. software)

Joomla – a free, open-source content management framework for publishing web content. It is built on a model-view-controller web application framework but can also be used independently. It is written in PHP, uses object-oriented programming techniques, and includes feature such as page caching, RSS feeds, printable versions of page, news flashes, and blogs. After WordPress, Joomla is the most used CMS on the Internet.

Link Strategy Plan – a marketing plan that is directly connected to the company's identity and goals

Magento – an open-source e-commerce web application, written in PHP

Marketing Automation Tools – software that performs simple, repetitive marketing tasks (i.e., email blasts). It saves time and decreases human error.

Marketo – a company specializing in marketing automation software

Measurables – anything that can be measured, such as sales, web traffic, back links, etc.

Multivariate Testing – a method of systematically testing a website page for its success in achieving the goals for that website by presenting the page in all its variations to website visitors. It will present the various elements differently (color, wording, image, etc.) as well as their placement on the page each time a new visitor comes to visit the website. Analytics will show which variation is most successful whether it be an increased user registration or a successful purchase.

Nichers – a business that offers something not offered by any other

Open Source Code – a computer program in which the source code can be modified by anyone. It is usually created collaboratively by programmers, who then share the changes with the general public.

PMP – Project Management Professional: a credential offered by the Project Management Institute, which certifies that the project manager is able to improve the success rate of projects by utilizing a set of principles set forth in the guide book put out by this Institute.

Positioning – a company's place in a particular market. For example, Smart Cars and Ferraris are both automobiles, however, one is known for being economical and the other is considered the epitome of luxury and adventure. They are "positioned" very differently in the market.

Proprietary Source Code – software that is exclusively licensed to a copyright holder, with a licensee given permission to use it under certain circumstances (for example, the licensee cannot share or modify it).

Qualitative Feedback – Qualitative Feedback is a body of observations and responses to one's work or performance that is based on comparisons and descriptions of characteristics in a non-numerical manner. Such feedback is often useful because it allows those giving the feedback to be more specific about what they do or do not like and what they believe could be improved.

Require-Docs – the project scope document that ML uses. A project scope document is a document that outlines the results that a project will produce and under what terms and conditions the service company such as ML will operate to perform their work. It is agreed to by both parties before the work is begun and can be altered as need be as the project changes.

Responsive Design – a website design that facilitates easy viewing, navigating and sizing across all devices (computers, tablets, smartphones, et cetera).

RFP – request for proposal. An invitation, put out by a client company, for vendors to bid on a project or contract.

SIX SIGMA – A set of tools and strategies for process improvement originally developed by Motorola in 1985." "Six Sigma is a highly disciplined process that helps us focus on developing and delivering near-perfect products and services." "Six Sigma is a fact-based, data-driven philosophy of quality improvement that values defect prevention over defect detection. It drives customer satisfaction and bottom-line results by reducing variation and waste, thereby promoting a competitive advantage.

Salesforce.com – a cloud-computing and social enterprise "software-as-service" company. Best known for its customer relationship management product, Salesforce.com also has several other social media integration, tracking and analytics products.

SCRUM - Scrum is an iterative and incremental agile software development framework for managing software projects and product or application development. Its focus is on "a flexible, holistic product development strategy where a development team works as a unit to reach a common goal" as opposed to a 'traditional, sequential approach.

SEM – Search Engine Marketing: a marketing plan that seeks to increase a website's ranking on search engines. SEM vendors include Google AdWords and Bing Ads.

SEO – Search Engine Optimization: relates to a website's ranking under search engines such as Bing or Google.

User interface – the user interface, in the industrial design field of human–machine interaction, is the space where interaction between humans and machines occurs.

W3C – The World Wide Web Consortium: an international community where Member organizations, a full time staff, and the public work together to develop protocols and Web standards.

Workflow – a sequence of connected steps of action where each action follows the previous without significant delay. Each step must be completed before the subsequent step can begin. It is a depiction of a sequential activity of operation of work as for a person or group of people working together or as part of the same end; one or more simple or complex mechanisms.

Index

www.ingramcontent.com/pod-product-compliance
Lightning Source LLC
Chambersburg PA
CBHW041310210326
41599CB00003B/57